BIG
BEHAVIORS
in small containers

131 Trauma-Informed Play Therapy Interventions
for Disorders of Dysregulation

Paris Goodyear-Brown, MSSW, LCSW, RPT-S

Published by:
PESI Publishing, Inc.
3839 White Ave
Eau Claire, WI 54703

Cover: Amy Rubenzer
Editing: Jenessa Jackson, PhD
Layout: Amy Rubenzer

ISBN: 9781683734673 (print)
ISBN: 9781683734680 (ePUB)
ISBN: 9781683734697 (ePDF)

Printed in the United States of America.

PESI Publishing
pesipublishing.com

About the Author

Paris Goodyear Brown, MSSW, LCSW, RPT-S, is one of the leading experts on the intersection of childhood trauma and play therapy in the world. In her groundbreaking model, TraumaPlay™, she integrates both directive and non-directive approaches to treatment into an umbrella framework that gives clinicians structure to employ evidence-informed interventions with confidence while encouraging creativity and freedom to follow the child's need all along the way in treatment. She is the clinical director and senior clinician of Nurture House, the executive director of the TraumaPlay Institute, a TedTalk speaker, an adjunct instructor of psychiatric mental health at Vanderbilt University, and a sought-after speaker.

Table of Contents

9   Care for Me 55

10   Conch Connections 56

11   Family Fun Fortune Tellers 57

12   Stick Together Ice Cubes 61

13   Who Knows Whom? 64

14   Rupture and Repair 67

15   Superhero Dyads 70

16   "I Value You" Valentines 72

17   "With Me" Water Bottles 74

18   Bejeweling Affirmations 76

19   I'm a Robot 77

20   Heartfelt Follow-the-Leader 78

Chapter Four: Understanding Our Stress Responses **79**

1   WOT Are You? 81

2   My Brain and My Window 84

3   Making My Window 86

4   Who Is Amy G. Dala? 87

5   What Is Amy G. Saying Now? 89

6   Soothing Amy G. 91

7   Embedding Amy G. 92

8   Maraca Madness 93

9   Balancing on the Head of a Pin 94

10   The Polyvagal Zoo 97

11   Sleuth the Sloth 100

12   Farmers and the Fainting Goat 101

Chapter Five: Enhancing Self-Regulation **103**

1   Personalized Pinwheels 105

2   Five-Count Breathing 108

3   Weighed Down 110

4   Modulate with Music 111

5   Yoga Tunes 112

Acknowledgments

I would first like to thank the growing community of TraumaPlay™ practitioners. As you absorb the core values and structure of the model, your questions have helped to further refine the framework, your wisdom has led to new innovations, and your individual and collective creativity have given rise to new interventions.

I am also so grateful to each of my play therapy colleagues who contributed interventions to this resource:

Paula Archambault, LMSW, RPT-S

Michelle Codington, MS, LMFT, RPT-S, CFPT

Helené Duerden, MBACP

Amy Frew, PhD, LMFT, RPT-S

Tonya Haynes, MMFT

Dora Henderson, LMHC, RPT-S, CST

Eleah Hyatt, MA, LMFT, RPT

Robert Jason Grant, EdD, LPC, RPT-S, ACAS

Tasha Jackson, LCSW

Carmen Jimenez-Pride, LCSW, RPT-S

Sueann Kenney-Noziska, MSW, LCSW, RPT-S

Neal King, LCSW

Liana Lowenstein, MSW, RSW, CPT-S

Clair Mellenthin, LCSW, RPT-S

Jessica Stone, PhD, RPT-S

Dayna Sykes, LPC-S, MHSP, RPT

Jennifer Tapley, MEd

Lindsey Townsend, LCSW

Tammi Van Hollander, LCSW, RPT-S

Christine Zouaoui, LPC, RPT-S

Introduction

I have had the great privilege of helping tiny humans and their caregivers (parents, teachers, daycare workers, school counselors, mental health providers, and others) stick together through hard things for over twenty-five years. Across the years and the diagnoses, one truth has stood out more than any other: The biggest behaviors can sometimes come in the smallest containers. A three-year-old who is having a full-blown tantrum because he doesn't have words to express his frustration (or isn't able to access the words yet), an eight-year-old who is bullying younger kids on the playground, an eleven-year-old who is having a panic attack as she thinks about the math test she will take later that morning—if any of these children resemble your client population, this book is for you.

Children who erupt in big behaviors often feel shame and guilt after an eruption. With our new understanding of the neurobiology of stress—how stress can originate in the body, be stored in the body, and be given shape in emotions, cognitions, and behaviors—mental health practitioners are better equipped than ever to help children and their caregivers come back to regulation more quickly. We can help children expand their adaptive coping repertoire to deal with these stress responses without engaging in big behaviors, and ultimately stay more grounded in themselves and better connected to those around them.

This book offers over 130 interventions designed by myself, the community of TraumaPlay™ practitioners, and other like-minded therapists. These interventions were developed in real-world environments (schools, clinics, residential treatment settings, in-home settings, and private practice settings) to help children with various diagnoses, including:

- Developmental trauma disorder

- Posttraumatic stress disorder (PTSD)

- Attention-deficit/hyperactivity disorder (ADHD)

- Oppositional defiant disorder (ODD)

- Anxiety disorders of all kinds

- Autism spectrum disorder

- Sensory processing disorder

- A range of mood lability disorders

What do all these diagnoses have in common? The likelihood of increased episodes of big behaviors, which can come in *acting out* or *acting in* forms. These behaviors occur with greater frequency, have greater intensity, and last longer than upsets experienced by other children. Therefore, children who exhibit big behaviors become outliers in their classrooms, their families, and their communities.

Acting Out Behaviors	Acting In Behaviors
• Hyperactivity	• Hopelessness/apathy
• Impulsivity	• Ruminating or perseverating thoughts
• Inconsolable crying	• Self-loathing
• Hitting others	• Low self-esteem
• Spitting, biting	• Dissociative behavior
• Throwing things	• Depression, numbing, slowing of responses
• Destroying property	• Freezing/death feigning
• Lying	• Withdrawal
• Stealing	• Addictions
• Cheating	• Suicidal ideation
• Panic attacks	• Self-injurious behavior (head banging, cutting, scratching)
• Chronic irritation	

I have worked with children who have exhibited each of these big behaviors and with some children—specifically, children with complex trauma histories—who have exhibited all of them. Over the course of the last twenty-five years of my work, a model has emerged for treating these children. The framework for this model was steeped in my first real job in the mental health field, which involved serving as the assistant counselor of a program for children with periods of intense dysregulation and chronic big behaviors. My actual job description included driving a van into inner-city communities, picking up children and teens from school at the end of the school day, driving them to our center for an hour-and-a-half of group treatment, and driving them home afterward. In actuality, though, my education about what trauma symptoms look and feel like began in the close quarters of that van. I watched as clients who had been fairly regulated during the treatment group began to escalate on the drive home, becoming increasingly dysregulated as we got closer and closer to home. It was as if their brains were catching on fire as we approached the source of their distress.

After years of tweaking, finessing, and rethinking the origins and underpinnings of these behaviors, I developed the scaffolding for a treatment program originally named Flexibly Sequential Play Therapy (Goodyear-Brown, 2010a). It consisted of key evidence-informed treatment components needed to help children with a history of trauma, as well as those who are angry, anxious, depressed, impulsive, rageful, embroiled in self-doubt, and mired in self-loathing. Recently renamed TraumaPlay (Goodyear-Brown, 2019, 2021), this umbrella model provides a framework of treatment goals that harnesses what we understand about the neurobiology of play and the neurobiology of trauma, and the power of one to heal the other. It provides a clinically sound, evidence-informed approach to treating big behaviors in children, building on what we understand in the field of childhood trauma to be best practices in treatment.

For example, most practitioners would agree that it is important to explore *how* a child client copes before delving into trauma-related content that might require them to engage in adaptive coping. Therefore, the treatment goals in this model cover seven broad areas that sequentially build on one another, making sure to sufficiently address each content area before moving on to the next. You may notice that most of these treatment goals line up with the chapters in this book:

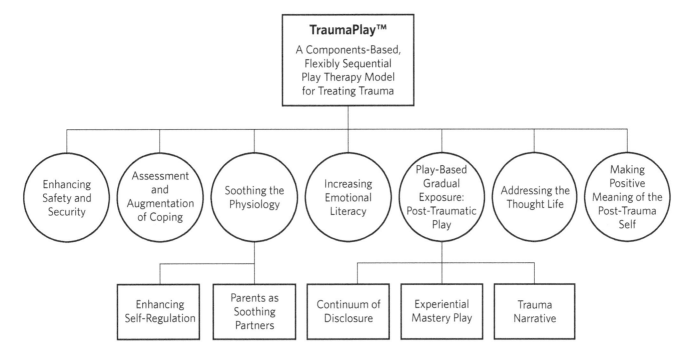

In addition, TraumaPlay values the therapist's role as a Storykeeper and invites the holding of hard stories in play and expressive arts. TraumaPlay therapists are always looking for playful ways to "bring it in the room," understanding that naming hard things in a matter-of-fact way can leach some of their emotional toxicity and mitigate any taboos or secrets around them. As part of this process, every TraumaPlay therapist works to embody three roles—the Safe Boss, the Nurturer, and the Storykeeper—and then transfers these roles to the parent or caregiver so they can safely hold their child within this three-part container. In the role of the **Safe Boss**, the adult functions as a co-regulating presence who provides healthy structure to the child, while the **Nurturer** provides the child with repeated instances of nurturing care. Finally, in the role of **Storykeeper**, the caring adult is tasked with keeping a coherent narrative of the child's story and connecting it back to the current big behaviors. Therefore, you will see these three roles referenced in various ways throughout the text.

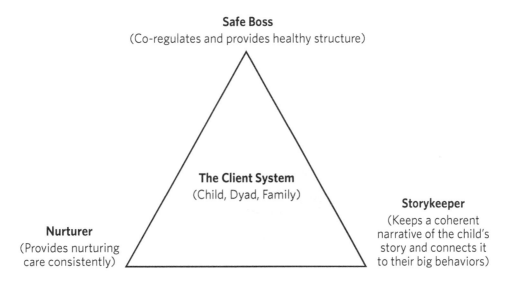

Whom This Book Is For

I expect that those using this book are mental health professionals who have advanced degrees and, for the most part, are licensed in their chosen fields. It is incumbent upon you, the treating professional, to position each intervention within a unique case conceptualization for each client. Clients can get stuck in the therapeutic process, especially when approaching content that is difficult for them to explore (e.g., their aggression, their anxiety, their awkwardness in social settings, or specific traumatic events). The play therapist's palette, shown below, is a tool that I developed as a kind of "quick guide" for clinicians to reference when a client appears to be stalled in treatment. For example, a therapist who has been using mainly cognitive interventions may need to offer more kinesthetic involvement. Or a client who has experienced therapy with such seriousness that it is overwhelming may benefit from the introduction of more humor and novelty into the mix.

When therapy appears to be stalled, the mitigators on the play therapist's palette can offer alternative ways to approach difficult content and can ultimately jump-start the treatment process. Individual clients may resonate more with some activities as opposed to others, and the more fun the interventions are for the client, the faster the behaviors can begin to shift. Ultimately, these precious young ones want their stories to be told, and they want to experience and have others experience their *goodness*. When children and teens have big behaviors, whether those are acting out or acting in behaviors, they tend to experience their badness.

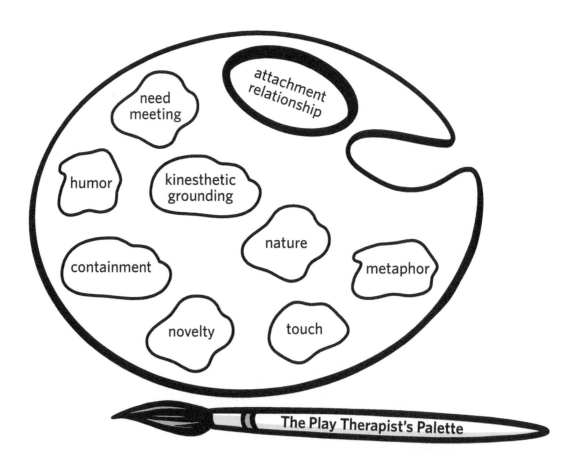

Reproduced with permission from *Trauma and Play Therapy* (Goodyear-Brown, 2019)

What Is in This Book

The book is divided into eleven chapters, each beginning with an explanation of the current evidence base for the particular treatment goal covered, followed by a host of fun, play-based interventions for therapists, yielding over 130 clinically powerful interventions. Many of the activities are accompanied by reproducible worksheets or handouts that can be immediately used in clinical practice, and some include illustrations to further clarify the directions and spark creativity.

Chapter 1 offers interventions for treatment planning, as goal setting is critical in determining which interventions are used, and when, in a continuum of treatment. In TraumaPlay, goal setting is related to positive behaviors we want to see the client or family grow in, as opposed to focusing solely on the cessation of current maladaptive behaviors. Our hope is to lay down new neural wiring and deepen existing pathways during the course of treatment.

Chapter 2 offers techniques for enhancing safety and security, since nothing more can happen clinically until this is accomplished. This chapter offers general guidelines for what qualifies as adaptive or maladaptive coping. The play-based activities that follow assess a client's current coping repertoire and provide strategies for identifying and enhancing adaptive coping.

Chapter 3 focuses on enhancing attachment, as TraumaPlay clinicians believe that the most important aspect of healing is our healthy attachments to others. Steeped in concepts from interpersonal neurobiology (Schore, 2003; Siegel, 2010), TraumaPlay practitioners are always going to work on enhancing the delight in the attachment relationship in tandem with enhancing a client's self-regulation and before processing anything harder (i.e., trauma content) that might require the scaffolding of a co-regulating caregiver or Safe Boss.

Chapter 4 provides playful psychoeducational activities to help children, teens, and their caregivers better understand their stress-response systems. These interventions provide a way to explore the concept of the window of tolerance with clients, as well as family-friendly ways to explain polyvagal theory and the neuroception of safety, danger, and life threat.

Chapter 5 builds on this expanded understanding by enhancing self-regulation through a multitude of play-based interventions grounded in mindfulness, breath work, and rhythm work. These activities are intended to help clients practice downregulating during periods of intense arousal and upregulating during moments of slowed responding.

Chapter 6 offers activities to increase impulse control and build attentional capacity, since children with big behaviors often have difficulty in these two areas. These play-based exercises provide clients with the practice and repetition they need to expand their ability to exert self-control and to delay immediate gratification. More specific interventions are also included to help manage anger and anxiety. For dysregulated youth, excitation, aggression, and anxiety can all balance on the head of a pin, neurophysiologically speaking (Goodyear-Brown, 2019). The more disinhibited a child becomes, the more sudden, startling, and potentially explosive their anger reactions will be. Therefore, interventions are also provided to help children manage big emotions and their resulting big behaviors.

Chapter 7 focuses on enhancing emotional literacy. When children don't have the words for their feelings, their emotions come out in their bodies. Therefore, the activities in this chapter help children identify their current feelings, expand their feelings vocabulary, enhance emotional granularity, identify situations that tend to engender different emotions, embrace the idea that people can experience several emotions at the same time, and understand that all of our feelings are welcome and useful to us.

Chapter 8 offers interventions that enhance social skills and self-esteem, as children with big behaviors often have trouble making and maintaining friendships, which can damage their sense of self-worth. These interventions help clients practice opening and closing circles of communication in prosocial ways while helping them feel more competent. These activities are broken down into playful "serve-and-return" interactions that help clients learn how to increase eye contact, read body language cues, share, use words to ask for what they need, and take the perspective of others.

Chapter 9 offers many cognitive behavioral play therapy interventions to address the variety of dysregulated thought patterns that are characteristic of children with big behaviors, including rigid thinking, negative self-talk, blame shifting, and incoherent narratives. This chapter provides an explanation of the cognitive triad—the relationship between thinking, feeling, and doing—and then breaks down activities that help clients identify cognitive distortions, engage in playful thought-stopping strategies, and create cognitive replacement statements, including "boss back" talk.

Chapter 10 invites caregivers to become more trustworthy Storykeepers for their children and provides interventions that will help clients increase the coherence of their narratives related to trauma, stress, or other hard things in their lives.

Finally, **chapter 11** prioritizes the making of a meaningful goodbye at the end of treatment. Many young clients with big behaviors live within family systems linked with multiple adverse childhood experiences (ACEs; Anda et al., 2006). Parents or caregivers come and go—sometimes to rehab centers, sometimes to jail—and sometimes they move in and out of availability to give care based on their own mental health issues. For all these reasons, TraumaPlay therapists want the termination process to be a corrective emotional experience in its own right, valuing the relationship that has been established and the hard work that has been accomplished.

When the biggest behaviors show up in the smallest containers, it can be overwhelming for the grown-ups tasked with caring for and helping these little ones. From the six-foot-tall dad who feels helpless in the face of his tantruming toddler who's a quarter his size, to the exhausted working mom who wants to scream right back at her raging teenager, the families we serve need help in dealing with dysregulation. This book offers new and innovative tools to help clinicians come alongside children, teens, and caregivers as they stick together through hard things. My hope is that with this book, you will feel better equipped to harness the power of playful interaction to enhance attachment, increase regulation, and provide healing connections for our most vulnerable clients.

Treatment Planning and Goal Setting

The smaller the container (the younger the child), the more confusing the big behaviors can be. Young children have limited abilities to use their words and are not yet able to reflect deeply on their own lived experience, making parent or caregiver involvement in the assessment phase critical. At the same time, the older the child or teen, the more complicated their treatment can be due to family, peer, school, and community influences—not to mention the tumultuous set of changes that happen in the brains and bodies of teenagers. Therefore, no matter the age of the minor client, it is critical to understand the origins, underpinnings, and reinforcers of the big behaviors prior to beginning treatment.

At Nurture House, the child and family treatment center that has been the home of TraumaPlay, clinicians engage in an extended assessment phase in order to create the most effective treatment plan for the client. We begin with a thorough biopsychosocial assessment with the parents or other primary caregivers, followed by dyadic assessment sessions that include the child as well. These assessments are followed by several play therapy sessions during which we engage in a play-based assessment of the client's current way of relating to the world, their current emotional literacy, their current coping repertoire, how they perceive their family dynamics, and how they perceive their big behaviors.

TraumaPlay therapists are always asking, in the presence of a big behavior, "What is the underlying need?" Once we have identified the need, the logical next question is "How do we meet the need?" The answer—and there may be multiple answers for any one client—helps to flesh out the treatment plan. The core components of TraumaPlay set forth in the introduction offer some scaffolding to help you create treatment goals, but careful case conceptualization is needed prior to implementing any of the interventions in the following chapters. Understanding where these various interventions fit within an overall continuum of treatment gives rise to the TraumaPlay mantra: *Follow the child's need*. In some cases, clinicians may need to begin treatment by helping caregivers shift their paradigms related to the big behaviors or reflect on their own attachment history more deeply to become co-regulating containers for their children (Goodyear-Brown, 2021). In other cases, helping the family better understand their stress-response systems and how they interact with each other may be most effective. In still other cases, the focus may need to be on an individual client's expansion of their self-regulation or anger management skills.

During this joining phase of treatment, it is also important for the client to have opportunities to engage in goal setting. It is common for caregivers to have different goals than their child has for themselves. Understanding what each person hopes to change and creating a shared treatment plan builds rapport and therapeutic trust while providing a road map for further treatment. The activities that follow are helpful in this work.

1.1 THE PROBLEM/THE PROBLEM ALL BETTER

DESCRIPTION:

This intervention is done with the caregiver and the child during the assessment phase of treatment. It helps you, the therapist, understand how each person perceives the distress in the system and what their perception of health and peace would look like in their family. Some family systems will be safe enough to do the intervention together and share their work with each other. With other systems, especially ones in which you believe that what the caregiver would share might be shaming, you may need to have separate sessions for the caregiver and the child, becoming the Storykeeper for each of them independently first.

TREATMENT GOALS:

- Assess the client's and the caregiver's perceptions of the clinical issue
- Help the client create a future template involving clinical change/growth
- Focus the client and caregiver on actionable steps toward change

MATERIALS NEEDED:

- Two copies of the *Bordered Frame* template
- One copy of the *Magic Wand* template (or an object that can serve as a magic wand)
- Scissors
- Coloring utensils

DIRECTIONS:

1. Invite the client to draw a picture of one problem related to the family system in the first frame.*

2. Once the client has completed this first drawing, have them draw a second picture in the other frame, giving the prompt "Draw a picture of the problem all better." Encourage the client to use their imagination.

3. Give the client a copy of the *Magic Wand* template and invite them to cut out the wand and, if they'd like, to decorate it. Or they can make their own wand. (You can even go on a nature walk and find a stick to paint in magical colors.)

4. Instruct the client to lay the wand between the two pictures (as a sort of bridge) and to write on the wand one action step they can take today toward resolving the problem.

---

*If the child is too young for or physically struggles with drawing, you can verbalize the problem and let the client wave the magic wand and talk about what would make it "all better."

BORDERED FRAME TEMPLATE

MAGIC WAND TEMPLATE

1.2 DEEPENING THE PATH

DESCRIPTION:

Children and their caregivers may need help shifting their paradigm about goal setting away from behaviors they want to stop seeing and toward behaviors they want to start seeing. Many families come into treatment with the goal of extinguishing the negative behavior. This intervention helps clients understand that change happens as new neural pathways are laid down and adaptive behaviors are strengthened through practice, rather than through making the goal the cessation of a behavior.

TREATMENT GOALS:

- Identify adaptive behaviors for therapeutic growth
- Help the client understand that practicing new skills helps create change

MATERIALS NEEDED:

- Kinetic sand tray
- *Deepening the Path* handout

DIRECTIONS:

1. Invite the client to run their pointer finger through the sand once. Watch as the sand slowly moves back into place.

2. Explain that the brain is a lot like the sand, or like tall grass:

   "When you walk through tall grass one time, it will bounce right back up. But when you walk through it over and over, it starts to lay down and a path is formed. The same is true in your brain when you try new things: If you do something once, it's not likely to 'stick' as something that works. But if you practice something over and over, a new neural path is formed and you can use that new behavior again."

3. Explain that you want to help them figure out what to do, not just what to stop doing. Clients will likely have already identified the goals in a negative way, such as *to stop lying*. For the child who comes from maltreatment or neglect, their lying may have been adaptive and stem from a place of being unable to trust others to meet their needs. In this case, the pathway you need to deepen might be stated as *risking telling the truth*. If the lying is an impulsive behavior of a child with ADHD, the pathway that may need to be deepened is *stopping to think before answering*. Become curious with the client and/or caregiver about which behaviors, thoughts, and strategies will create new pathways or strengthen current ones.

4. Give the client the *Deepening the Path* handout and have them write the behavior they want to strengthen in the path. In many cases, new pathways of responding may need to be identified for both the caregiver and the child or teen.

DEEPENING THE PATH HANDOUT

When you walk through tall grass one time, it will bounce right back up. But when you walk through it over and over, it starts to lay down and a path is formed. The same is true in your brain when you try new things: If you do something once, it's not likely to "stick" as something that works. But if you practice something over and over, a new neural path is formed and you can use that new behavior again.

Write the pathway you want to deepen, or practice, in the path below. This might be a behavior that helps you build relationships with other people, like using your words to ask for what you need. Or it might be a behavior that helps you feel calm, like taking a deep breath before you respond to someone else's words or actions.

1.3 PAVING THE PATH

DESCRIPTION:

After a long-term treatment goal has been concretized with the *Deepening the Path* handout, caregivers and clients need help breaking down this goal into shorter-term, actionable objectives. This intervention offers a tool for setting short-term treatment goals.

TREATMENT GOALS:

- Create short-term goals for treatment
- Break down therapeutic goals into actionable steps

MATERIALS NEEDED:

- Kinetic sand tray
- Miniature stepping-stones
- Completed *Deepening the Path* handout (from activity 1.2)
- *Paving the Path* handout

DIRECTIONS:

1. Using the same kinetic sand tray from the *Deepening the Path* activity (1.2), remind the client that the kinetic sand slowly started encroaching on the path they had made with their finger. Invite the client to create a new path in the sand, but this time add stepping-stones to keep the sand held back.

2. Once the client has added the stepping-stones, explain that the stepping-stones are like the small steps they will take toward change. Discuss actionable steps for treatment (growing self-regulation skills like deep breathing, noticing their self-talk without judging it, etc.). These actionable steps are framed as paving practices.

3. Lastly, give the client a copy of the *Paving the Path* handout and have them complete it. It is most helpful if the caregiver can be available for this session, as some of the steps may involve them.

ADAPTATION FOR TELEHEALTH:

Many children and teens enjoy building in the digital worlds of Minecraft™. Clients can make paths in Minecraft and use this game platform for developing treatment goals and actionable stepping-stones to those goals.

PAVING THE PATH HANDOUT

The deepened pathways will be more defined if the stepping-stones pave the way. List a paving practice (an adaptive behavior) for each stone.

GOAL: _____

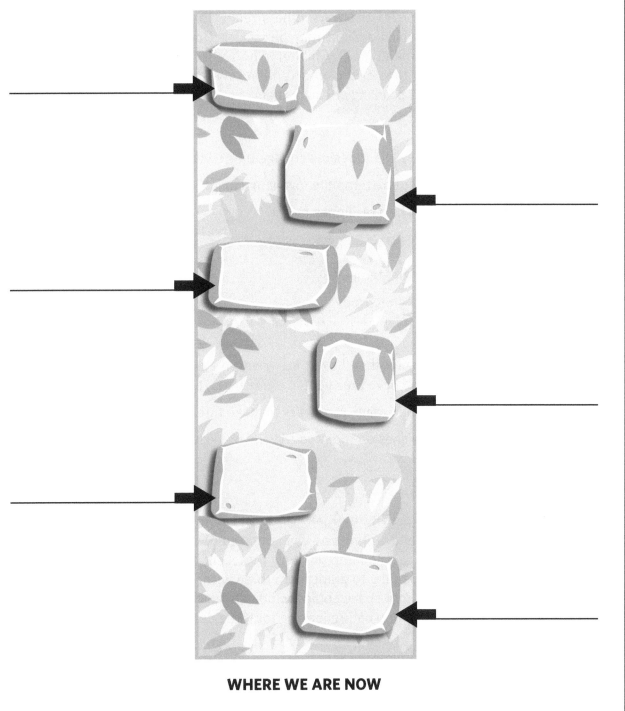

WHERE WE ARE NOW

1.4 THREE WISHES

DESCRIPTION:

Children with big behaviors experience a lot of correction, and they may already believe themselves to be stuck in negative cycles of interactions with others. Offering a wish fulfillment prompt can open up clients' imaginations and solutioning capacities for other ways of relating to others or for the ways others relate to them. This intervention can also help identify areas in which a client may be lacking (for example, a child with food insecurity may wish for unlimited food). Children who are living in situations that need to change may also take advantage of this intervention to wish for these changes (such as asking for their parents to stop yelling at each other).

TREATMENT GOALS:

- Assess areas in which the client desires change or growth

- Help the client create a future template involving clinical change/growth

- Harness the imagination as a resiliency factor

MATERIALS NEEDED:

- *Magic Wand* or *Wizard's Hat* template

- A magic wand or wizard's hat prop

DIRECTIONS:

1. Invite the client to imagine they have been given magical powers. Offer the magic wand or wizard's hat, and have the client imagine being a wizard.

2. Invite the client to use their magical powers to make three wishes.

3. Write down the three wishes on the *Magic Wand* or *Wizard's Hat* template, becoming the wizard's scribe.

VARIATIONS:

Change this to a hands-on activity by making a wand from a wooden dowel, attaching three pieces of ribbon to it, and writing one wish on each of the ribbons. A fun alternative prompt involves offering a genie's lamp, inviting the client to rub the lamp, and asking them to imagine a genie appearing to grant them three wishes. Or, use a dandelion as the prompt for wish fulfillment. Your space could include an adhesive dandelion placed on the wall, or you could venture out into nature looking for three dandelions to blow.

MAGIC WAND TEMPLATE

Write your wishes in the magic wand!

WIZARD'S HAT TEMPLATE

Write your wishes in the wizard's hat!

1.5 GOALS FOR GROWTH

DESCRIPTION:

Many children with big behaviors are sensory seekers and are more open to cognitive work, like goal setting, when it is paired with a full-body activity, such as basketball. Kinesthetic involvement can also mitigate the approach to hard things. Basketball gives the therapist, caregiver, and child a joint focal point so that intense eye contact is avoided during goal setting.

TREATMENT GOALS:

- Assess areas in which the client and the caregiver need therapeutic growth

- Provide kinesthetic involvement to mitigate a hard conversation

- Use the process of playing basketball as a parallel for setting therapeutic goals

MATERIALS NEEDED:

- Outdoor basketball hoop and basketball (or an over-the-door miniature basketball hoop and toy basketball)

- *Goals for Growth* template

- Scissors

- Coloring utensils

DIRECTIONS:

1. Invite the client and caregiver to play basketball, taking turns with the therapist.

2. After some play, become curious about the steps involved in successfully getting the ball in the basketball hoop. These might include (1) focusing attention, (2) readying the body, and (3) following through with fluid action.

3. Explain that the same process is important in setting therapeutic goals: The work of shifting big behaviors will require focused attention, body-based regulation and mindfulness, and follow-through on action steps by both the caregiver and the child. Help the caregiver and the child each identify two goals for treatment.

4. Invite the client and caregiver to cut out the basketballs from the *Goals for Growth* template, write their goals under the basketballs, and color them as desired.

GOALS FOR GROWTH TEMPLATE

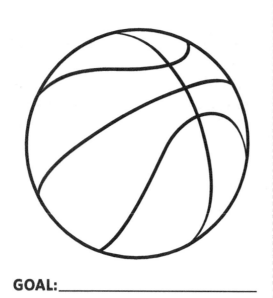

GOAL:_____

_____

_____

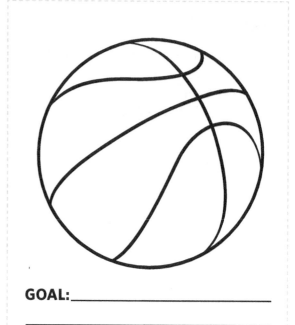

GOAL:_____

_____

_____

GOAL:_____

_____

_____

GOAL:_____

_____

_____

1.6 BRIDGING THE GAP

DESCRIPTION:

Many children with big behaviors have an easier time expressing things symbolically instead of linguistically. This intervention offers the boundaried projective space of the sand tray as a way for children to explore where they are now, where they want to be, and one step they can take toward their goal. This can be done with an individual child or teen, or with a caregiver if a sand tray is provided for each participant.

TREATMENT GOALS:

- Assess areas in which the client desires therapeutic growth
- Help the client engage in right-brain articulation of a goal
- Identify one therapeutic step toward the goal

MATERIALS NEEDED:

- Sand tray
- Miniature bridge
- Variety of other miniatures

DIRECTIONS:

1. Invite the client to explore the sand tray miniatures.
2. Ask the client to choose a miniature to represent one problem or big behavior with which they struggle, and place it on the left-hand side of the sand tray.
3. Ask the client to choose a miniature to represent the therapeutic growth or change they want to experience, and place in on the right-hand side of the sand tray.
4. Invite the client to place the bridge in between the two symbols.
5. Encourage the client to reflect on the symbols chosen, and find a third symbol to represent one small action step they can take right away to work toward the change they wish to experience.
6. Take a picture of the sand tray before dismantling it, as this will be a useful right-brain reference for this treatment goal.
7. This process can be repeated for multiple treatment goals or at intervals throughout the treatment process as the client accomplishes action steps.

Enhancing Safety and Augmenting Adaptive Coping

The first component of TraumaPlay is enhancing safety and security. The second is assessing for and augmenting adaptive coping. These two goals go hand in hand. Children with big behaviors must perceive that you enjoy and accept them (even in their dysregulation) before they will feel safe enough to begin taking risks to try out new behaviors or to even believe that new ways of responding to distress are possible.

Child-centered play therapy (CCPT), an evidence-based approach, is the first tool we use to begin to enter a child's world and better understand their heads and hearts (Baggerly et al., 2010). Play is the language of children (Landreth, 2012) and children can show and tell us things through their play that would be difficult for them to access linguistically. Play is the safest way to begin a relationship with a child, and the interventions in this book are woven into the fabric of sessions that are grounded in play. Within the play, we see how they cope with entering a new environment (our office space), interacting with new people (us), and exploring new objects (the toys). A more structured assessment of the client's current coping repertoire follows. It is best practice to understand the ways a child copes with big emotions or difficult content before we approach any of the treatment issues more deeply.

If we find that a client has very few adaptive strategies, we help the client tease apart which coping strategies are helpful to them and which may be maladaptive or hurtful. We also help the client understand that coping solutions that may have been adaptive for them during a traumatic event (or while in the care of an unsafe caregiver) may no longer be needed. Finally, we work in playful ways to identify and practice adaptive coping tools so these will be available to them later in the therapeutic process.

During the working phase of treatment, a client's stress-response system is often triggered while engaging with difficult content, and it is useful to have a whole toolkit of healthy coping strategies available.

Generally speaking, clients are served best by coping strategies that help them access their Safe Bosses when needed. Moving the client toward social supports seems to be more helpful than engaging in strategies that isolate them. Finally, this chapter ends with a tried-and-true strategy for adaptive coping, which involves creating a three-dimensional safe place for the client that can become an internalized image they can use to counteract stress.

THE COPING TREE

DESCRIPTION:

Big behaviors are often an indicator that a child or teen's repertoire of coping strategies is limited. When children have experienced trauma, they may have developed coping strategies that served them well in surviving that environment. This intervention offers a playful way to assess the client's current adaptive and maladaptive coping strategies.

TREATMENT GOALS:

- Assess the client's current coping strategies, both adaptive and maladaptive
- Help the client reflect on their current coping repertoire and identify places of growth

MATERIALS NEEDED:

- *Coping Tree* handout
- *Coping Tree Apples* template, scissors, and glue (or apple stickers in various sizes)

DIRECTIONS:

1. Invite the client to pretend they are an apple farmer. Use the following script: "Imagine that some of the apples fall from the tree and are not picked up quickly enough. It rains, and they lay there for a while. What's going to happen to those apples?" Children will say they are going to get mushy, get worms, or rot. "Imagine the apples on the tree ripen and get plucked at just the right time. What will these be used to make?" Children enjoy generating the list of apple pies, apple juice, apple fritters, and so on.

2. Let the client know that the apples on the tree represent adaptive coping strategies, and the apples on the ground represent maladaptive ones. If the child has experienced a specific traumatic event, you can ask, "When you think about the scary thing that happened, what do you do?" If the big behaviors seem to stem from a more global activation of the stress-response system, ask, "When you are feeling really stressed, what do you do?" Glue an apple on or under the tree for each answer given. You want to fully exhaust the client's current coping repertoire before you start processing individual coping strategies. Larger apples can represent strategies they use a lot, and smaller apples can be used for ones they use less frequently.

3. Help the client reflect on how useful each coping strategy is now, and explore both adaptive and maladaptive strategies.

ADAPTATION FOR TELEHEALTH:

Using a drawing tool (such as the Zoom whiteboard), share your screen so you and the client can make a coping tree collaboratively in the digital environment.

COPING TREE HANDOUT

Put an apple on the tree for each healthy way you cope when you are stressed. Put an apple on the ground for each unhealthy way you cope when you are stressed.

COPING TREE APPLES TEMPLATE

Cut out the apples and use them to represent your coping strategies. Use the larger apples for the things you most often do to cope, and use the smaller apples for the things you do less often.

2.2 COPE CAKES*

DESCRIPTION:

Children who are easily dysregulated need practice in using adaptive coping when they feel stressed. Some children do not know the difference between helpful coping choices and harmful ones. This intervention translates the adult coping literature into developmentally sensitive terms for children and provides scaffolding for the creation and practice of adaptive coping strategies.

TREATMENT GOALS:

- Teach the child four healthy "ingredients" for adaptive coping
- Identify adaptive coping strategies that include these four ingredients
- Practice adaptive coping strategies in multiple environments
- Celebrate the coping strategies that are most effective

MATERIALS NEEDED:

- *Mixer*, *Baking Tin*, and *Cope Cake* templates
- Decorative materials for either paper or actual cupcakes

DIRECTIONS:

1. Explain that healthy coping involves four ingredients: It should (1) be good for you, (2) be good for others, (3) be easy to do, and (4) help you feel better. Using the *Mixer* template (or a play mixer if you have one available), list one ingredient on each of the mixing blades.

2. Using the *Baking Tin* template, help the client (and the caregiver, when possible) identify six coping strategies that include all four ingredients. If available, a miniature play baking tin and mini cupcake liners can be used instead.

3. Instruct the client and caregiver to practice these coping strategies at home for the next few weeks, becoming detectives together about which ones are most helpful.

4. Have a celebration in which you cut out a paper cope cake from the *Cope Cake* template and decorate it with glitter glue and sequins. Alternatively, bring in actual cupcakes** and invite the family to decorate them with icing, sprinkles, and so forth, celebrating the growth of the client's adaptive coping repertoire.

---

*Adapted from *The Worry Wars: An Anxiety Workbook for Kids and Their Helpful Adults* (Goodyear-Brown, 2010b).
**Check with the caregiver in advance for food allergies.

MIXER TEMPLATE

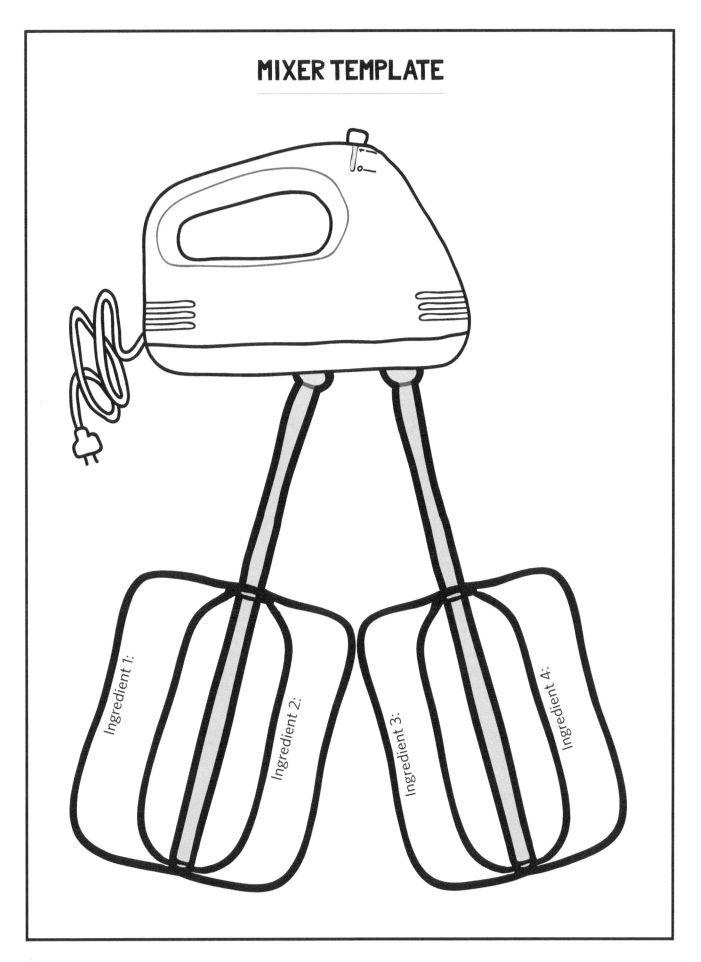

Ingredient 1:

Ingredient 2:

Ingredient 3:

Ingredient 4:

BAKING TIN TEMPLATE

COPE CAKE TEMPLATE

2.3 COPING KABOBS*

DESCRIPTION:

Children who are easily dysregulated need co-regulation by their Safe Bosses more frequently than their peers do. This intervention offers a playful way for children to identify their co-regulators and the coping strategies that effectively harness the co-regulating relationship.

TREATMENT GOALS:

- Identify the client's Safe Bosses (co-regulating caregivers)
- Explore adaptive coping strategies that utilize the client's co-regulators

MATERIALS NEEDED:

- Wooden dowels or fondue sticks
- Pieces of fruit (e.g., grapes, apple slices)**
- Marshmallows

DIRECTIONS:

1. Explain to the client that when you are feeling wobbly (dysregulated), you need a stronger foundation or scaffolding to lean on to help you stay upright.

2. Invite the client to stack fruits and marshmallows on top of each other, making a tower. Eventually it will get too tall and topple over.

3. Invite the client to try using a dowel or fondue stick as a reinforcing center that can support the foods as they are stacked on top of one another.

4. Identify Safe Bosses (co-regulating caregivers) who are strong enough for the client to lean on, just like the fruit and marshmallows lean on their support system.

5. List coping strategies that require their Safe Boss, such as reading together, baking together, or getting a hug when the client is feeling stressed.

---

*Created by Helené Duerden, UK TraumaPlay supervisee.
**Check with the caregiver in advance for food allergies.

2.4 THE COPING CAVE

DESCRIPTION:

Children with attachment trauma have often learned that people can hurt you and are not to be trusted. When they needed a caregiver to accurately read their cues and meet their needs the most, these children were abandoned, even hurt, by the very person who was supposed to comfort them in their fears. In the face of this powerful paradox, children develop coping that is often independent of the caregiver, learning how to meet their own needs and comfort themselves. This can lead to isolation, addiction, and dissociative strategies. This intervention helps explore these dynamics.

TREATMENT GOALS:

- Help the client reflect on coping strategies that served them during previous traumatic events or chronic stressors
- Validate that learning to meet your own needs can be a form of protection
- Explore the potential pitfalls of isolation-based coping strategies
- Explore which of the client's previous coping strategies are still adaptive and which can be let go of now

MATERIALS NEEDED:

- Sand tray
- Miniature cave
- Variety of other miniatures
- *Coping Cave* handout

DIRECTIONS:

1. Allow the client to explore the miniature cave and invite them to choose its placement in the sand.

2. Invite the client to choose a figure to represent a younger version of themselves and to place it inside the cave.

3. Explain that when children have been hurt by people who were supposed to take care of them, some children learn to protect themselves by doing things on their own, by never asking for help, and by disconnecting from the real world. Normalize and even celebrate how smart this young child was to figure out a way to stay safe at the time. Explain that caves offer shelter from storms and from predators, but that if we stay in the cave all the time, we will not have access to everything we need.

4. Invite the client to choose objects to represent coping strategies that connect them to others and put these in the sand tray. Then have the client choose objects to represent coping strategies that isolate them from others and put these in the cave.

5. The *Coping Cave* handout can be used adjunctively or instead of the sand tray to concretize both adaptive and maladaptive coping strategies.

COPING CAVE HANDOUT

Think about coping strategies you have used and choose an object that can represent each strategy. Place the coping strategies that connect you to others outside the cave. Place the coping strategies that isolate you from others inside the cave. If no miniatures are available, pictures can be drawn instead.

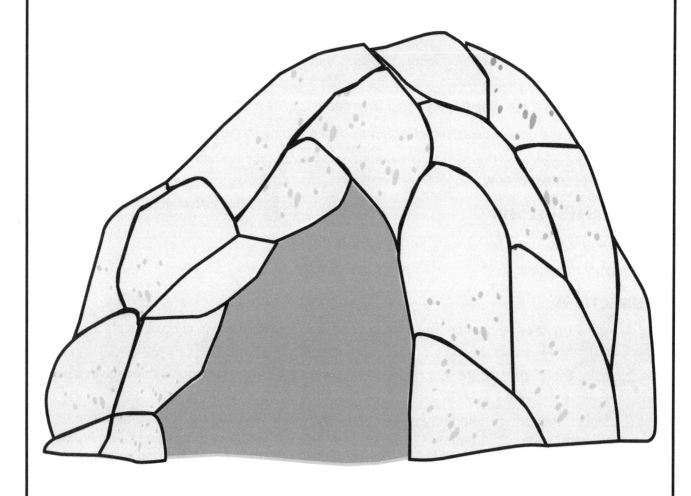

COPING MENU

DESCRIPTION:

Children with big behaviors often have sensitive sensory systems. When they start to feel stressed, anxious, or angry, they can benefit from coping strategies that harness the power of our five basic senses in order to self-regulate. This play therapy intervention offers a template for helping clients individualize a sensory-soothing set of strategies.

TREATMENT GOALS:

- Explain the power of our five senses in helping us to self-regulate
- Identify sensory-soothing experiences in each of the five senses
- Offer shared mindful sensory experiences from their menu in session if time allows

MATERIALS NEEDED:

- Play food and dishes
- *Coping Menu* handout

DIRECTIONS:

1. Begin by engaging the child in a pretend meal, using play food and play dishes to pretend that you are at a fancy restaurant together. Decide together on an appetizer, a soup or salad, a main course, a side dish, and a dessert.

2. Explain that our sensory experiences can be comforting in the same way that a nice meal can comfort us.

3. Introduce the *Coping Menu* handout, starting with the appetizer. Ask the client, "What's just a little taste of something that helps you feel good and safe on the inside?" Invite the child to visualize (with their eyes closed, if clinically appropriate) and describe what it is about that food item that helps them feel that way, such as the item's texture, its temperature, or a positive memory they associate with that food. Have the client write the name of the food item in the corresponding space on the handout.*

4. Continue to make your way through the rest of the menu together, asking the same questions for each of the senses.

5. Explain to the child how they can bring up these mindful sensory experiences the next time they feel stressed or anxious.

---

*As a way to reinforce the sensory experience, the clinician could provide a small item to eat, such as a Hershey's Kiss® (check with the caregiver in advance for food allergies). You can have a mindful experience together, noticing the weight of it in your hand, the glint of the light against the silver wrapper, the sound of the crinkling foil, the smell of the chocolate, and so on. If you are trained in EMDR, bilateral stimulation can be used adjunctively to further install this sensory experience.

VARIATION:

Aspects of the *Coping Menu* can be extended to other environments with the caregiver's help. For example, if a child identifies that the silk edge of their baby blanket provides tactile soothing, a little square of it can be cut off or the caregiver can help the client find a similar piece of silk to keep in their pocket at school. When the child is anxious, they can simply reach into their pocket and touch this sensory-soothing anchor.

COPING MENU HANDOUT

Name something that helps you feel good and safe on the inside for each part of the meal.

Appetizer:
TASTE

_____
_____
_____

Soup/Salad:
TOUCH

_____
_____
_____

Side Dish:
SMELL

_____
_____
_____

Main Course:
SEE

_____
_____
_____

Dessert:
HEAR

_____
_____
_____

COMMUNITY CROWN

DESCRIPTION:

Children with big behaviors often need more co-regulation than their peers. Identifying supportive people in their school, home, faith, and extracurricular environments is one way to provide more opportunities for coping through connection.

TREATMENT GOALS:

- Identify support people in each of the client's environments
- Create a visual reminder of all the co-regulators in five different areas of social support

MATERIALS NEEDED:

- One or more copies of the *Support People* template
- Scissors
- Construction paper
- A stapler or tape
- Coloring utensils

DIRECTIONS:

1. Cut out at least five individual paper people using the *Support People* template.

2. Ask the client to identify one person who fills each of the following roles for them.* For each role, invite the client to color in a paper person to look like their real-life support person and/or write that person's name on the paper cutout.

   The client should identify someone who:

   a. gives them good, safe touches that help them feel good and safe on the inside

   b. says nice things to them or about them that help them feel good about themselves

   c. spends good time with them and helps them feel important

   d. helps them learn how to do something better or do something new

   e. they like to hang out with

3. Cut one or more strips of construction paper and fasten the ends together, forming a crown that fits on the client's head. Attach the paper people to the crown. The client can wear this home and put it on as needed to remind themselves of their support people.

---

*You may notice that the first three roles reflect several of the love languages (Chapman, 1992): physical touch, words of affirmation, and quality time. The fourth role is based on the need for children to experience competence building in order to feel good about themselves. The fifth role is related to the research-backed idea that when a child has even one positive, supportive peer relationship, they are protected from all sorts of psychopathology in the world. Additional people can be added.

SUPPORT PEOPLE TEMPLATE

33

2.7 SAFE PLACE SAND TRAY

DESCRIPTION:

Many children with big behaviors have histories of maltreatment or neglect and may not have experienced felt safety in any environment. For this reason, we never ask a child to remember a place that they felt safe but, rather, have them create or imagine a place where they could feel safe. Creating safe places in the boundaried space of the sand tray allows for clients to touch and feel the scene, visualizing the final product externally and then potentially internalizing this image for retrieval during stressful moments.

TREATMENT GOALS:

- Assist the client in creating a three-dimensional safe place

MATERIALS NEEDED:

- Sand tray and miniatures
- Modeling clay or coloring supplies

DIRECTIONS:

1. Introduce the idea of imagining a place where the client could feel safe.

2. Invite the client to create this safe place scene in the sand tray.

3. Using the script provided, help the client augment their experience of this created safe place by exploring the sensory impressions they experience as they imagine being in their safe place:

   "I want you to think about a safe place. This is a place where you feel safe, secure, comfortable, and peaceful. It can be a place you make up in your head or an actual space that exists somewhere. Once you have thought of a safe place, please create it in the sand tray using whatever figures you need. If you can't find exactly what you need, you can make a symbol out of clay or draw a picture that can be placed in the sand tray."

4. Once the client has created a safe place, begin exploring this space: "Tell me about your safe place." If the client has chosen a figure to represent themselves, use the following prompts:*

   a. Imagine that you are there, in your safe place.

   b. What can you hear in your safe place? Smell? Taste? Touch?

   c. What emotions do you experience in your safe place?

   d. What thoughts do you have in your safe place?

---

*If you are trained in EMDR, you can further install each of these sensory experiences, emotions, and positive cognitions with slow, short sets of bilateral stimulation. Sometimes as you enhance aspects of the safe place, children notice something they didn't before, so give time and room for new ways of noticing.

2.8 CREATING YOUR DIGITAL SAFE PLACE*

DESCRIPTION:

Although the components of safety can have general themes, what calms, soothes, and provides safety to a child can be very individualistic. Creating and identifying the components of a safe, soothing environment can be instrumental for a client who needs to employ any level of self-soothing. This intervention utilizes the therapeutic powers of Digital Play Therapy™ to highlight this process through the Virtual Sandtray App. This app can be utilized in session while communicating and processing material and in generalizing this knowledge to other areas of the client's life.

TREATMENT GOALS:

- Assist the client in identifying soothing, calming elements that can contribute to a sense of safety

MATERIALS NEEDED:

- A tablet (preferred) or smartphone with the therapist version of the Virtual Sandtray App installed

DIRECTIONS:

1. Prompt the client to create a scene that feels unsafe.

2. Prompt the client to create a second scene that includes calming, soothing, and safe elements.

3. Compare and contrast the elements in each scene.

4. Identify the calming, soothing, and safe elements depicted.

5. Discuss (1) how the client can visualize a similar scene when needed to calm themselves and create a sense of safety and (2) how the client might create a safe place in their real life that mirrors elements in their safe scene.

ADAPTATION FOR TELEHEALTH:

You and the client will each need a tablet (preferred) or smartphone with the Virtual Sandtray App installed; the client should install the free client version. You will both log in to the app and connect remotely.

*Created by Jessica Stone, PhD, RPT-S.

2.9 POSTCARDS IN MOTION

DESCRIPTION:

Clients with big behaviors can have difficulty relaxing. This intervention offers a titrated approach to relaxation, inviting clients to identify a vacation spot, visualize it, write about it, and ultimately engage in full-body work surrounding their experience of this fun, safe place. If a client really enjoys this activity, you can create an entire book of postcards over several sessions, with each postcard focusing on experiences, both safe and unsafe, that are tied to specific locations.

TREATMENT GOALS:

- Assist the client in identifying or creating a vacation destination
- Expand the client's experience of their vacation destination by pairing expressive arts and full-body engagement

MATERIALS NEEDED:

- Blank pre-cut postcards or the *Postcards* template
- Coloring utensils

DIRECTIONS:

1. Invite the client into a guided imagery exercise using the following prompt:

   "Choose a fun, safe place where you would like to go for vacation. This might be a place you have actually been to, a place you have seen in pictures or movies, or a place that you create in your mind."

2. Give the client a blank pre-cut postcard or the *Postcards* template.

3. Invite the client to draw a picture of their vacation destination on the front of the postcard.

4. Have the client imagine being in this vacation spot. Ask them what they can hear, see, taste, touch, and smell in this place.

5. Ask the client to identify a special person to whom they would like to send a postcard from this vacation spot. Have the client write the person's name on the postcard.

6. Invite the client to write two to three sentences describing their vacation spot to this special person.

VARIATION:

For older children or teenagers, this activity can be expanded by having the client engage in full-body work after they create their postcard.

1. Ask the client to label a separate piece of paper with the numbers 1–4. Help them visualize their vacation spot a second time.

2. Then have them list the following aspects of this special place: (1) an architectural element, (2) a small detail, (3) a main element (the thing that sticks out the most to them), and (4) the mood or feeling of the place.

3. After the client has made their list, ask them to pair a full-body gesture with each of the four elements, and then put these gestures together in order. The resulting movements form a kind of dance.

4. Invite the client to repeat the sequence of gestures (dance) while you read their postcard out loud.

POSTCARDS TEMPLATE

Dear _____,

three

Enhancing Attachment

The attachment relationships between a baby and their earliest caregivers shape the ways in which that tiny human will relate to others for a lifetime. In utero, a baby's symbiotic relationship with their mother provides them with their first full-body experiences of safety or distress. Babies are, in a very literal sense, connected to their mothers.

This attachment relationship continues as the child enters into the world. When babies are born, they instinctually cry out for hunger and connection. If these signals are quickly interpreted and responded to by the caregiver, the baby learns that these needs will be met. This reinforces the idea that connection is safe and good, and resource and relationship become paired in healthy ways. The parent delights in the baby, even in their neediness. In TraumaPlay, the term *Nurturer* is used for caregivers as they provide thousands of repetitions of nurturing care to their little ones.

As babies develop into toddlers, they begin to need boundaries for their own safety. At some point, the child hears their first *no* spoken firmly by a caregiver. This *no* can feel like a sudden rupture to the relationship. The caregivers must set a boundary safely and provide ongoing connection, as well as make a repair when this is needed (Siegel, 2010). In TraumaPlay, *Safe Boss* is the term we use for caregivers when they set limits or structure a child's experience or expectations in a way that supports ongoing attachment.

Therefore, caregivers are the most important co-regulators for their children (Siegel & Hartzell, 2013). They offer children both a secure base (a place from which a little one can explore) and a safe haven (a place to which a little one can return when in distress) (Bowlby, 1988). The younger the child is when big behaviors occur, the more important the co-regulating caregiver becomes. However, these behaviors are often so big that caregivers are exhausted when they enter treatment, and patterns of reciprocal delight have been sucked out of the system. For this reason, this chapter offers a multitude of attachment-enhancement activities that increase both the quality and the number of delighting-in interactions that happen between the caregiver and child, helping clients experience connections as safe and pleasurable. Many of these intervention activities provide playful, low-risk situations in which caregivers can fill the roles of Nurturer and Safe Boss for their children with the support of a therapist.

While these interventions can be especially helpful in working with foster and adoptive caregivers, attachment disruptions also happen in biological families due to addiction, a parent's own mental health issues, a child's neurodivergent brain development, or traumatic events. Regardless of the source of the attachment disruption, relational trauma requires relational healing. Attachment disruptions often show up in big behaviors first, making the attachment-enhancement interventions a foundational part of the healing process.

3.1 AIRPLANE LOVE NOTES

DESCRIPTION:

When a child is chronically dysregulated, their caregivers may spend more time correcting the child's behaviors than they do delighting in the child. This intervention offers a playful way for the caregiver and child to give positive affirmations to each other. Both partners follow step-by-step instructions to create the airplane. Affirmations are written on the airplanes and flown to each other.

TREATMENT GOALS:

- Facilitate positive communication loops between the caregiver and child
- Increase the number and frequency of affirmations given to the caregiver and child
- Practice following step-by-step instructions to enhance executive function

MATERIALS NEEDED:

- Standard (8.5" × 11") pieces of paper
- Writing utensils

DIRECTIONS:

1. Offer the caregiver and child each a piece of paper and walk them through the following directions:

    a. Fold the paper in half lengthwise, then reopen it.

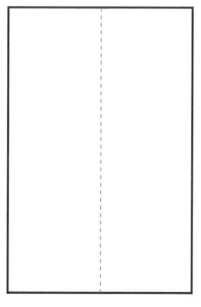

b. Fold the top left and right edges of the paper into the middle, forming a triangle at the top of the paper.

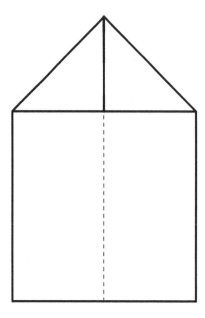

c. Fold the bottom left and right edges of the triangle into the center, and run your thumb along the creases to secure them.

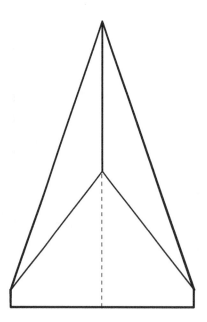

d. Fold the now triangular paper in half, along the center crease you made before.

e. Fold the top layer in half again, bringing the two longest sides of the triangle together. Flip the paper over and repeat on the other side. Press along the creases.

2. Instruct the caregiver and child to open the last crease and to write a positive affirmation or something they love about each other.

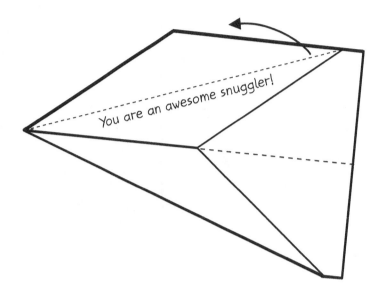

3. Have the caregiver and child practice flying the airplanes toward each other. When the child receives the caregiver's airplane and reads the note, they can write a note in response. This process can happen as many times as the dyad likes, opening and closing positive circles of communication.

4. Encourage the caregiver to begin sending the child Airplane Love Notes at home, surprising them by flying one into their bedroom while they're playing with building blocks, into the bathroom as they're brushing their teeth, and so forth.

3.2 LOVE LINKS

DESCRIPTION:

Children with big behaviors often get more attention for their troubling behaviors than for their positive choices. This disproportionate focus on negative behavior can lower clients' self-esteem and create distance in their relationships with caregivers. This exercise encourages caregivers to celebrate their child's positive qualities and to concretize their child's helpful choices.

TREATMENT GOALS:

- Increase the number and frequency of positive communications between the caregiver and child

- Practice verbal and written affirmations in the family system

- Encourage the opening and closing of circles of communication within the family system

MATERIALS NEEDED:

- *Love Links Sentence Starter* template, pre-printed on various colors of paper, or simply construction paper (a different color for each family member)

- Markers

- Scissors

- Tape or staples

DIRECTIONS:

1. Invite the caregiver-child dyad or the whole family to create Love Links together.

2. Give each participant several pieces of construction paper (or several copies of the *Love Links Sentence Starter* template), allowing each person to choose a different color paper to write their contributions on. Have them cut their paper into long, rectangular strips (or cut out the strips on the template).

3. Ask the caregiver to think of one character trait, positive attribute, or act of kindness that they appreciate about their child. Have the caregiver write their statement down on one love link. Have them curl the love link up and tape or staple the ends together. Then have them read it out loud to the child or family members.

4. Invite the child to talk about their experience of how it feels to hear this affirmation from the caregiver. If the child is not able to articulate this verbally, see if they can demonstrate their feelings through their facial expression. You can also verbalize the nonverbal responses you see in the child's body: "Johnny smiled really big when you told him how much you enjoy his..."

5. Invite the child to similarly identify one character trait, positive attribute, or act of kindness they appreciate about another family member and to add that link to the chain.

6. Send the Love Links home with the family, playfully challenging them to create the longest chain they can during the week and to bring it back next session for you to see.

I like the way you ...

It was really helpful when you ...

You are ...

LOVE LINKS SENTENCE STARTER TEMPLATE

I like the way you...

It was really helpful when you...

You are...

3.3 STICK TOGETHER BOOKMARKS

DESCRIPTION:

Children and caregivers both benefit from reminders of the strength of their attachment relationship, especially when they are separated from each other. The idea that we can stick together with our loved ones even when we are physically separated is a profound truth. This intervention offers a reminder of this truth and is especially helpful for children with separation anxiety.

TREATMENT GOALS:

- Provide attachment enhancement
- Create transitional objects for both the caregiver and child to use during times apart
- Amplify the power of the caregiver and child's connection even when they are separated

MATERIALS NEEDED:

- Duct tape of various colors and patterns
- Scissors
- Permanent markers

DIRECTIONS:

1. Invite the client and caregiver to explore your duct tape collection together.

2. Ask them each to choose a roll of duct tape that represents their personality.

3. Cut two pieces of each type of duct tape (all pieces should be the same length). Create two bookmarks, one for the caregiver and one for the child, by having them slowly and carefully press the sticky side of the child's tape together with the sticky side of the caregiver's tape to form a bookmark. If they go too quickly, they are likely to get wrinkles. Compare this slow, cooperative work to the work it took to build their connection.

4. Affirm that this connection is not severed when they are separated from each other.

5. Invite each partner to write an affirmation on the other's bookmark.

6. Invite them to use the bookmarks whenever they are apart from each other.

STICK TOGETHER LIGHT-UP TOWERS

DESCRIPTION:

Children who go back and forth between two homes can often manifest the stress of these transitions in their behaviors, having big behaviors for the first hours or days after the transitions. Play therapy offers children the chance to make more coherence of the stressful events in their lives. This activity, which involves playing with light-up blocks, offers a special way for children of divorce to process having two homes.

TREATMENT GOALS:

- Provide a transitional object for the child who has trouble managing separations from their caregivers
- Help the caregiver and child verbalize positive affirmations with each other
- Encourage focus on relational appreciation to enhance attachment

MATERIALS NEEDED:

- Light-up blocks

DIRECTIONS:

1. Invite the child to play with the blocks. Explain that the blue blocks have a power connection, and let the child watch as you plug one end into the block and the other into the wall.

2. Children instantly become curious—if they place another block on top of that one, will it light up? The answer is yes, as long as the shiny silver edges are touching each other closely enough. Several blocks can be placed on top of each other, all lighting up, but eventually the child reaches the edge of what that circuit can hold.

3. Explain that there are several blue bases, and a separate light-up tower can be made with the remaining blocks. Invite the child to create an additional tower with these blocks.

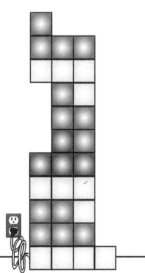

4. As they create these two beautiful pieces, begin to explore the comparison between their two homes and the two towers.

5. Affirm that sometimes the best way to have all the blocks functioning together is to build two separate structures.

LOVE CONNECTORS

DESCRIPTION:

This intervention is near to my heart, as my son Nicholas created it. When he was four, I was packing for a speaking trip, and he was watching me when he suddenly blurted out, "We need more love connectors!" I wasn't sure what he meant, but I used my tried-and-true reflection skills and said, "We do need more love connectors! Let's go find some." I let him lead the way around the house until he found two identical hair ties. He put one on his wrist and one on mine and said, "These will be our connectors. Don't take it off." The next day, as I was dropping him off at preschool, we were holding hands as we walked in. Our wrists were touching and he said, "Look, Mommy! Our love connectors are powering up." That night, as I video called him from my hotel room, we touched our wrists together through the screen, powering the love connectors up again for the next day of being apart. These transitional objects that communicate connection are very important for our young children.

TREATMENT GOALS:

- Create transitional objects that represent the strength of connection during times of separation

MATERIALS NEEDED:

- Pipe cleaners (or any material from which you can make bracelets) in various colors

DIRECTIONS:

1. Offer the pipe cleaners to the caregiver-child dyad.

2. Instruct the child to choose a color and the caregiver to choose a complementary color.

3. Give the caregiver and child two pipe cleaners—one of each chosen color—and have them twist the two strands together to form a bracelet.

4. Identify times of separation during which they will wear their love connectors.

5. Decide on times to video call during the time apart to "recharge" the connectors.

3.6 | NURTURE NECKLACES

DESCRIPTION:

Children with separation anxiety may scream, cry, cling, or have symptoms that mirror a panic attack when they are forced to leave their caregiver. Offering a transitional object, something concrete that is a connection to the caregiver, can help children cope during separations. This intervention provides a playful way to do this while also rehearsing shared positive memories that strengthen family identity.

TREATMENT GOALS:

- Provide a transitional object for the child who has trouble managing separations from their caregivers
- Rehearse shared positive memories
- Enhance connection during times of separation

MATERIALS NEEDED:

- String or jewelry wire
- Beads (various colors and shapes)

DIRECTIONS:

1. Introduce the materials for jewelry making.
2. Invite the caregiver to choose a bead and string it on the wire. Encourage the caregiver to tell a "delighting-in story" of a shared memory with their child as they add the bead.
3. Invite the child to choose a bead, string it on the wire, and share a memory of a fun or positive time with their caregiver.
4. Continue to lead the dyad in taking turns telling stories that include nurturing, connected experiences between them while stringing the beads that represent these memories.
5. Explain that their memories are part of what connects them when they are apart.

VARIATION:

The memories can also be represented by colors of sand placed into mini sand-art bottles, which are then made into necklaces to be worn during separations.

3.7 LONGTIME LOVIES

DESCRIPTION:

Children with big behaviors who have experienced early neglect or maltreatment may not have a template for nurturing care. They may have a stuffed animal that they cling to and that may have come with them into a foster or adoptive home. They may like the way it smells and the way it feels, and they may anchor to it in moments of stress. The constant use of the stuffed animal can result in rips and tears. Taking care of these hurts on the stuffed animal can help traumatized children learn that there is help available for their hurts as well.

TREATMENT GOALS:

- Model nurturing care with a stand-in for the hurt child

- Support the role of the caregiver as a Safe Boss and trustworthy helper

- Practice telling stories about hurts, in preparation for the child's trauma narrative work

MATERIALS NEEDED:

- A favorite lovie, blankie, or stuffed animal

- Needle and thread

- Bandages, lotion, or other first-aid supplies

- A Safe Boss caregiver

DIRECTIONS:

1. Ahead of session, ask the caregiver and child to examine the child's lovies at home and to bring in one that has a hurt.

2. Invite the caregiver to tenderly look over the stuffed animal and to process out loud what might be done to help. If the help will require sewing up an area that is torn, explain that since needles are sharp and can hurt the child, the caregiver will help supervise the threading of the needle. Children with aggressive behaviors at home or school may especially benefit from having their self-control and safe use of the needle in the session celebrated and tied to the co-regulating presence of the Safe Boss.

3. Once the lovie has been nurtured, invite the caregiver to notice any hurts that may be on the child's body and to offer ways to help (bandages, lotion, etc.).*

---

*The therapist should stick close together with the caregiver and child throughout the activity and take every opportunity to highlight the child's safe use of the needle. While the sewing repair is happening, the therapist engages the caregiver in storykeeping with questions such as, "Will you tell me about how your child first got their lovey? When and where do they spend time with their lovey?" If certain developmental time frames emerge, the therapist can elicit other delighting-in stories from the caregiver about that developmental age.

3.8 COMFORT CREATURES

DESCRIPTION:

In our modern world, children are separated from their caregivers for all sorts of reasons, including divorce, deployment, work that requires travel, and before- and after-school care when caregivers work long hours. As children run out of the energy required to regulate themselves, they need their co-regulators. When a co-regulator isn't available, a transitional object can help make the separation more tolerable, providing a part of the caregiver and a reminder of the caregiver's connection to the client even when they are physically separated.

TREATMENT GOALS:

- Create transitional objects that help children navigate separations from their caregivers
- Provide sensory anchors for the felt presence of the child's caregivers

MATERIALS NEEDED:

- Pom-poms
- Pipe cleaners
- Googly eyes
- Construction paper or felt pieces
- Scissors
- Glue
- Essential oils*

DIRECTIONS:

1. Explain to the client that it is normal to miss a caregiver when you are separated from them. Explore the times when your client misses their caregiver the most.

2. Explain that you will be making Comfort Creatures to keep the child company when they are missing their caregiver.

3. Invite the client to choose a pom-pom to be the body of their creature. Offer googly eyes of different sizes, pipe cleaners that can act as antennae, and felt pieces or construction paper to cut out for feet or hands.

4. Offer a variety of essential oils and ask the client to choose one or more scents that they associate with their caregiver. Add drops of these oils to the creature. (These get absorbed by the fuzz of the pom-poms and add to the sensory encoding of the transitional object.)

---

*Check for allergies before using any essential oils.

5. Invite the client to name each comfort creature (they may have one for when they are separated from each caregiver), to place it in a resealable plastic baggie, and to take it out to hold and play with it whenever they miss their caregiver the most.

6. Ask the caregiver to hold the comfort creature, infusing it with lots of love, before each separation.

3.9 CARE FOR ME*

DESCRIPTION:

There are many ways people express and receive nurturing. For some people, particularly children who have experienced attachment ruptures, trauma, or neglect, the concept of recognizing, acknowledging, and meeting needs can be foreign. This intervention utilizes the therapeutic powers of Digital Play Therapy to highlight this process through the game *Adopt Me!* on Roblox™.

TREATMENT GOALS:

- Assist the client in recognizing, acknowledging, and meeting needs, both as a nurturer and the one receiving the nurturing

MATERIALS NEEDED:

- A smartphone, tablet, or computer with Roblox (which can be accessed through a downloadable app or a web browser) for each participant
- A primary caregiver-approved, child-safe Roblox account for each participant

DIRECTIONS:

1. Log in to Roblox and find *Adopt Me!* either on the main page or via the search function.

2. Join via a private server to be in the world alone with your client(s) or via the main game play arena. Either way, join your client or have them join you so you are in the same world/server.

3. Have at least one player assume the role of a parent and at least one assume the role of a baby. The parent can bring the baby around in a stroller.

4. During the gameplay, the baby will have needs that must be met, such as food, drink, shower, nap, fun, and school.

5. Play the game while verbalizing the needs of the baby, meeting the needs, and making any appropriate parallels to the client's experience.

6. Switch roles as deemed appropriate for the client's needs.

*Created by Jessica Stone, PhD, RPT-S.

3.10 CONCH CONNECTIONS

DESCRIPTION

Children with acting out behaviors typically receive correction more frequently than they receive affirmation. This intervention helps to amplify the loving words of a caregiver to their child, and vice versa, while giving the child a transitional object associated with the caregiver's love that will be there even when they are separated.

TREATMENT GOALS:

- Provide a transitional object for the child who has trouble managing separations from their caregivers

- Help the caregiver and child verbalize positive affirmations with each other

- Encourage focus on relational appreciation to enhance attachment

MATERIALS NEEDED:

- Large conch shell (a big one from the ocean if you have one)

- Smaller conch shells (these can be purchased in bulk at a craft store)

- Paints and brushes

DIRECTIONS:

1. Show your large conch shell to the caregiver-child dyad. Explore any experiences they have related to hunting for shells at the beach, collecting shells, and so forth.

2. Ask each person to hold the shell up to their ear and listen. They are likely to say they hear the ocean. You can also share your experience of hearing the ocean in the shell.

3. Explain that the shell used to be with the ocean all the time, and it absorbed the sound of the ocean. Even though the conch is no longer in or near the ocean, it still retains the sound of the ocean.

4. Offer a basket of shells to the caregiver and child and ask them to each choose one. Once they have chosen their shells, explain that you want them to create keepsakes for the other to have when they are apart.

5. Invite them to each paint their shell for the other.

6. Have the caregiver speak words of affirmation, love, and hope for their child into their shell and give it to the child.

7. Ask the child to hold the shell to their ear and to bring those words back up in their mind and heart.

8. If appropriate, have the child speak affirming words into the shell they painted and give it to their caregiver.

9. Explain that when they are apart and miss each other or need some encouragement, they can hold up their shell and remember their loved one's words.

3.11 | FAMILY FUN FORTUNE TELLERS

DESCRIPTION:

When a child becomes easily dysregulated, a disproportionate amount of family time can be spent managing hard moments. Upsets, correction, and co-regulation can take enormous amounts of time. It can be helpful to have intentional doses of connected, enjoyable family time. This intervention helps caregivers and kids collaborate on fun group activities and implement protected times for connection.

TREATMENT GOALS:

- Increase positive interactions between the caregiver and child
- Enhance connection among the family members as they share novel experiences together

MATERIALS NEEDED:

- Paper (standard 8.5" × 11" printer paper, or you can use square paper and skip steps 1–2)
- Scissors
- Markers (or other writing utensils)

DIRECTIONS:

1. Take a piece of paper and pull the bottom edge up to the far-right edge, creasing the paper to create a triangle.

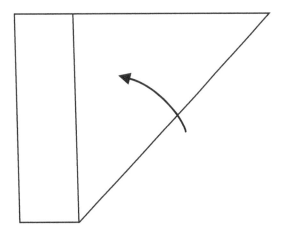

2. Cut off the extra paper to create a square.

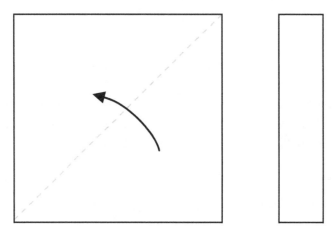

3. Unfold the paper, then fold it into a triangle and crease again, in the opposite direction as before. When you unfold the paper again, the creases should form an X.

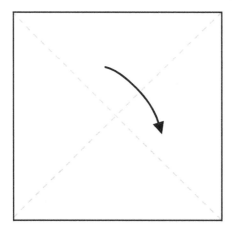

4. Bring the corners into the center of the paper and crease. Hold the tips of the triangles in place in the middle until all four are folded into a square.

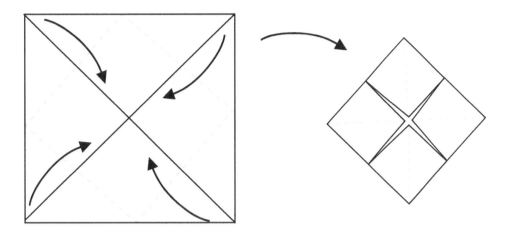

5. Flip the paper over, and fold each corner to the middle one more time.

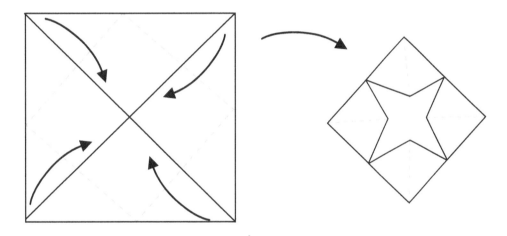

6. Write a different number on each smaller triangle, for a total of eight numbers.

7. Turn the fortune teller back over and write a color on each larger square, for a total of four colors.

8. Underneath each number, write a playful, connecting activity such as: trying out new restaurants, doing a baking project, coming up with silly snack ideas, watching a movie together, playing strategy games, solving puzzles together, playing a board game together, or going on a hike.

9. Encourage the family to pick one day a week where they will use the Family Fun Fortune Teller to plan some family time together.

   a. One person operates the fortune teller by sliding their thumbs and fingers under the four squares in a pincer-like way, and alternately moving their hands apart/together and their "pincers" open/closed.

   b. Another person chooses a color, then a number, as the person with the fortune teller moves it that number of times (for a word, use the number of letters it contains). With the third choice, open that flap on the fortune teller to reveal the corresponding activity.

STICK TOGETHER ICE CUBES*

DESCRIPTION:

Children with a narrowed window of tolerance for distress can have big behaviors as a response to everyday chores, like brushing their teeth or getting dressed. Caregivers may need to provide more co-regulation at these times. This technique helps clients understand the benefits of sticking together in difficult times. It encourages healthy connection and flexibility in thinking and responding to each other.

TREATMENT GOALS:

- Increase the client's connection to their feelings, thoughts, and relationships
- Equip the client with language to express their thoughts and feelings about family dynamics
- Identify ways in which the client can build connection with their family members

MATERIALS NEEDED:

- Four to six very frozen ice cubes**
- A paper plate
- *Stick Together Ice Cube Stack* template

DIRECTIONS:

1. Remove a few frozen ice cubes from the freezer and place them on the paper plate.

2. Ask the client to try to stack the ice cubes on top of one another. When the ice cubes are frozen, the client will not be able to stack them very high. Discuss with the client why the ice won't stack or stay stacked in place.

3. Next, allow the ice cubes to melt for a minute and have the client try to stack the ice cubes again. The ice cubes will stick together more easily, and a higher stack will be achieved. Discuss with the client what has changed and why the ice cubes will stack and stick together.

4. Using the *Stick Together Ice Cube Stack* template, ask the client to write down some activities they do with their caregiver (such as driving to school, doing homework, or getting ready for bed). Write those on the ice cubes.

---

*Created by Amy Frew, PhD, LMFT, RPT-S.

**Be aware of the client's sensory responses to temperature and texture. It may be helpful for clients to become comfortable interacting with the ice prior to starting the activity. It is also important to be aware of any history the client might have with using ice as a form of self-harm. This activity may be triggering and/or corrective in the client's history with ice.

5. Help the dyad think of ways to "melt" and stick together when they have difficult moments (such as creating a silly song together to sing while driving, having dance breaks during homework time, or creating a nighttime ritual back rub). Write those on the melted parts of the ice cubes.

6. You can also think of kind and connecting statements ("Let's stick together," "It's melting time," etc.) and write those around the ice.

STICK TOGETHER ICE CUBE STACK TEMPLATE

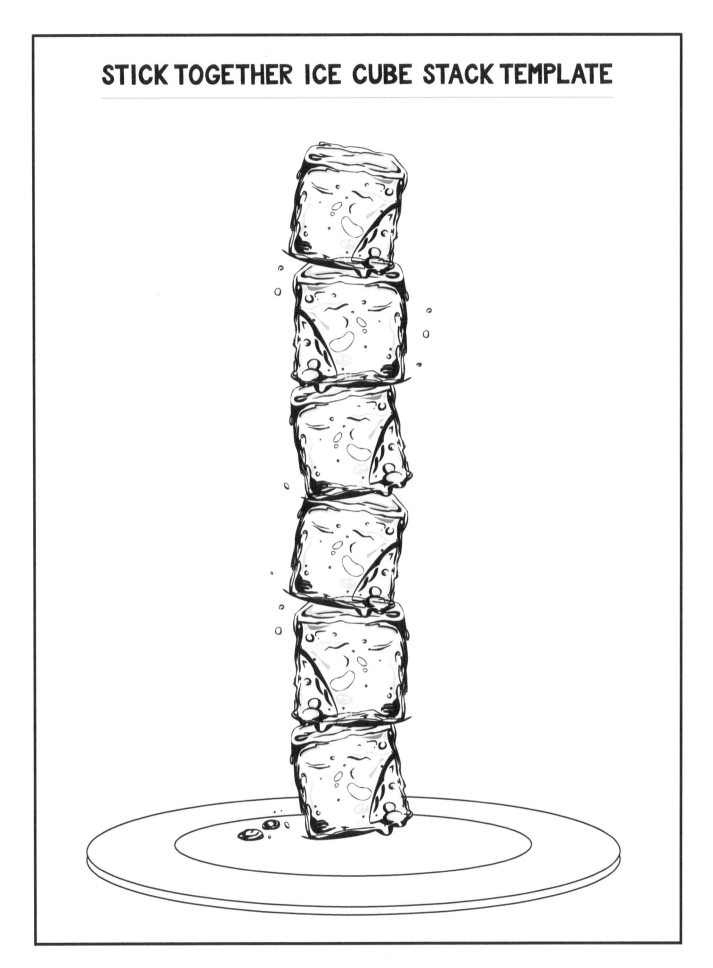

WHO KNOWS WHOM?*

DESCRIPTION:

It is important to offer moments that help create opportunities for connection and co-regulation, especially when you are working with clients and their caregivers together and big behaviors (such as aggression, debilitating anxiety, or noncompliance) are present in the family. As families work through the questions, they may find a new appreciation for each other. The ability to speak about positive memories is a nice way to help with co-regulation and create new connections.

TREATMENT GOALS:

- Increase the connection between the client and their caregiver and/or family members
- Identify ways in which the connection between family members exists

MATERIALS NEEDED:

- A piece of paper and a writing utensil for each participant
- Paper for you to keep track of each person's answers
- *Who Knows Whom? Cards* template, printed and cut out ahead of time

DIRECTIONS:

1. Decide who should take part in the game: the client and their caregivers or the entire family.

2. Give each person a sheet of paper and a writing utensil. Have them fold or draw divider lines on the paper so there's a section for each participant. Then ask them to write each person's name—including their own—in one of the sections.**

3. Explain the game to the participants: "We are going to ask questions about each other. Some will be about simple things, like 'What is your favorite food?' And some will be a little more complicated, like 'What was your favorite trip as a family?'"

4. Explain that each person should write the answer to every question—both the questions about their family members and the questions about themselves—on the paper by that person's name.

---

*Reprinted with permission from *Healing with Creativity: When Talking Just Isn't Enough* (Zouaoui, 2018).
**Children who may find writing daunting can draw symbols or pictures to represent their answers; another option would involve cutting many images from magazines prior to the session and inviting the client to choose from these pictures.

5. Pretending to be the host of the show, say, "Welcome to the Who Knows Whom Game! We have here [*child's name*] and [*caregiver's name*], and they will be writing answers about each other on their paper! The first question is... [*read the question card*]. Write your answer about [*name the person or people they need to write the answer for*]."

6. If there are several family members playing, have each player write each member's name (e.g., mom, dad, sister) on their paper. Each player writes down the answer they think the other members would give under their respective name.

7. Players can share their answers with each other after each question, or they can save all their answers until the end of the game.

8. When the game is over, help the dyad or family group reflect on what they have learned about each other.

WHO KNOWS WHOM? CARDS TEMPLATE

Card 1

What is this person's favorite color?

What is this person's favorite thing to do as a family?

Card 2

What is this person's favorite candy (or dessert)?

What is something this person always says to me?

Card 3

What is this person's favorite flavor of ice cream?

What is/was this person's favorite toy?

Card 4

What is this person's favorite animal?

How does this family member share love with others?

Card 5

What is this person's favorite pizza topping?

What was this person's favorite family vacation (or outing)?

Card 6

What is this person's favorite TV show (or movie)?

What is something this person wishes your family did more often?

3.14 RUPTURE AND REPAIR

DESCRIPTION:

When a child is engaging in big behaviors, their stress-response system has kicked into high gear. There may be yelling, crying, hitting, and name-calling. Caregivers may also lose their cool and have trouble co-regulating the escalated child. These moments are ruptures in the relationship. Boundary ruptures happen continually in families, but when a rupture involves hurtful words or actions, or withdrawal of affection, it is critical that repair be brought to that moment. When ruptures happen over and over and there is no repair, these become toxic ruptures that can create disconnection, as if the caregiver and child are on opposite sides of a chasm and can't get to each other. This intervention helps the caregiver and child practice naming the hurt and taking steps to repair it. Note that this intervention should be carefully placed in a continuum of treatment in which safety and rapport have already been deeply established.

TREATMENT GOALS:

- Explore individual actions that have caused a rupture in the caregiver-child relationship
- Assist the caregiver and child in owning their part of the rupture
- Identify steps, in both words and actions, that each person can take to make repair

MATERIALS NEEDED:

- *Rupture and Repair* template
- Writing utensils
- Scissors
- Stapler

DIRECTIONS:

1. Explain that in all families, caregivers and children have moments in which they become so stressed that they act in ways that hurt each other. Ask the caregiver and the client to each think about a time when they did or said something hurtful to the other. Explain that making repair involves both words and actions.

2. Offer them each a copy of the *Rupture and Repair* template. Have them write their name on one side of the heart and the other person's name on the other side. Then have them cut out both the heart and the "How do we repair?" strip of paper.

3. Have them cut the heart in two pieces along the middle line and staple each piece of the heart to either end of the "repair" strip. Have them offer words to make repairs, such as "I'm sorry I refused to get in the car and made us late" or "I'm sorry I called

you a name." Helpful apologies are specific and name the hurtful action. Write down the apology under "words."

4. Explore together what acts of restitution are meaningful to the other person. For example, if the refusal to get in the car cost the caregiver fifteen minutes of time, the child can offer to do a chore (e.g., washing dishes, making coffee) that would give the caregiver that time back. If one sibling has scratched the other, they may need to take care of the hurt with a bandage. Write down the agreed-upon actions to complete the activity.

RUPTURE AND REPAIR TEMPLATE

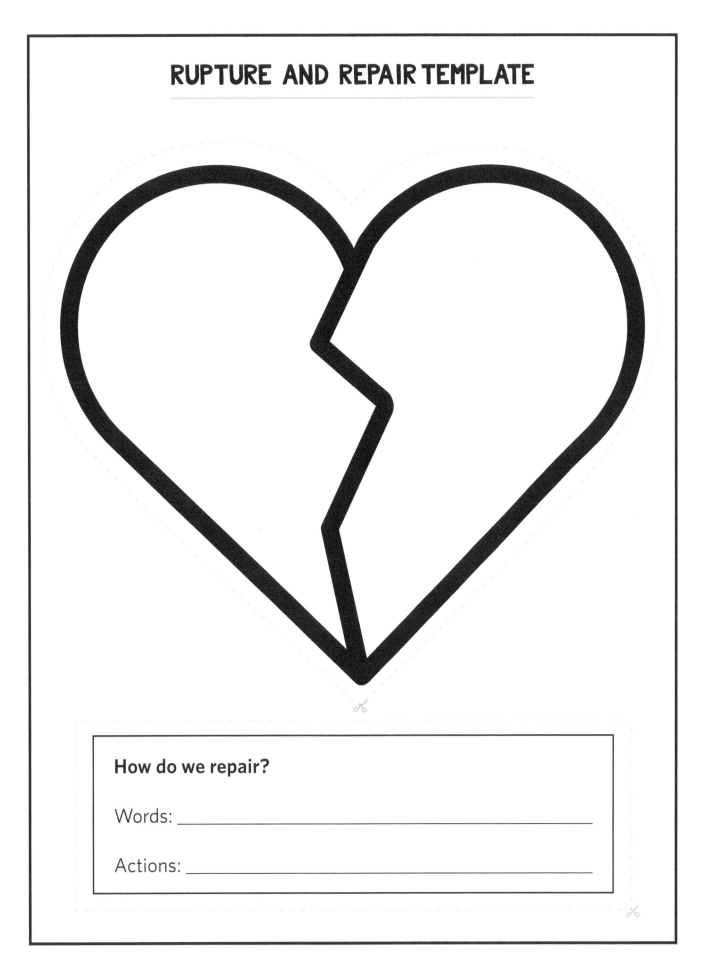

How do we repair?

Words: _____

Actions: _____

3.15 | SUPERHERO DYADS

DESCRIPTION:

Talking about the big behaviors that are happening within a family system is sometimes necessary, but it can trigger the child into a shame spiral. Especially when sessions are happening through telehealth, it is important to read the client's body language during difficult conversations. When the child's body gives us cues that they may be escalating, they are probably feeling polarized from their caregiver. This intervention is a quick way to bring connection back to the system.

TREATMENT GOALS:

- Increase the dyad's experience of being on a team together

- Expand the dyad's sense of positive connection

- Encourage the use of imagination to enhance each participant's sense of competence

MATERIALS NEEDED:

- Superhero costume pieces or materials to make them (e.g., foam, felt, or fabric pieces, scissors, glue)

- Camera

DIRECTIONS:

1. Explain that the caregiver and child are going to become superheroes! Explore with each partner what they want their superhero name to be and what superpowers they have. Make sure their powers amplify each other's, and talk about how they are more powerful together than apart.

2. Invite the caregiver and child to make their own superhero costumes or choose from costumes you've provided, then take a picture of them posing together. Lots of silliness and shared laughter ensues during this dress-up, creating a moment of shared delight with the caregiver and child.

3. Print or save the superhero picture and share it with the dyad as a reminder of their shared power when they stick together as a team. Explore the kinds of things they can do more easily together than apart.

ADAPTATION FOR TELEHEALTH:

Have the caregiver and child position themselves on the screen in superhero poses. Ask permission to take a screenshot of them and then share the image back through the screen. Use a drawing tool (like the annotate feature in Zoom) to draw superhero accessories on the picture of the dyad. Save and share the picture with them.

*photo edited to protect client confidentiality

3.16 "I VALUE YOU" VALENTINES

DESCRIPTION:

The attachment relationship is at risk when a child has big behaviors. Sometimes the caregiver is the source of anxiety that is being translated into dysregulation in the child. Other times the child's out-of-control behaviors trigger a caregiver's need to control the child and may result in repeated power struggles within the dyad. Increasing positive interaction between the caregiver and child is an effective way to begin restoring delight and trust in these systems. This intervention helps rewire the system to anticipate affirmations instead of conflict.

TREATMENT GOALS:

- Increase each partner's awareness of positive attributes in the other
- Increase the number of positive interactions between the caregiver and child
- Provide an in vivo experience of the caregiver verbally rehearsing the client's positive attributes

MATERIALS NEEDED:

- *"I Value You" Valentines* handout
- Heart-shaped Valentine's Day chocolate box
- Paper candy wrappers (or parchment paper cut into small squares)
- Pencils

DIRECTIONS:

1. Begin two weeks before the holiday by introducing the worksheet. Offer one copy to the caregiver and one to the child. Have each of them record one positive quality, characteristic, or act of kindness of the other each day until the next session.

2. At the next session, offer actual heart-shaped candy boxes, and have them rewrite the affirmations on the blank candy wrappers as they take turns sharing affirmations for each other verbally. If appropriate, offer candy to set inside each wrapper in the box.

3. Invite them to take turns reading each wrapper out loud to their partner. The boxes and wrappers can be taken home to be read again and again.

4. You might send additional wrappers home with the dyad so they can add to their boxes at home.

5. Caregivers can also be encouraged to surprise the child by putting an affirmation wrapper (and something small and sweet) into their lunch box intermittently.

"I VALUE YOU" VALENTINES HANDOUT

Each day, write down one positive quality, characteristic, or act of kindness that you appreciate about _____.

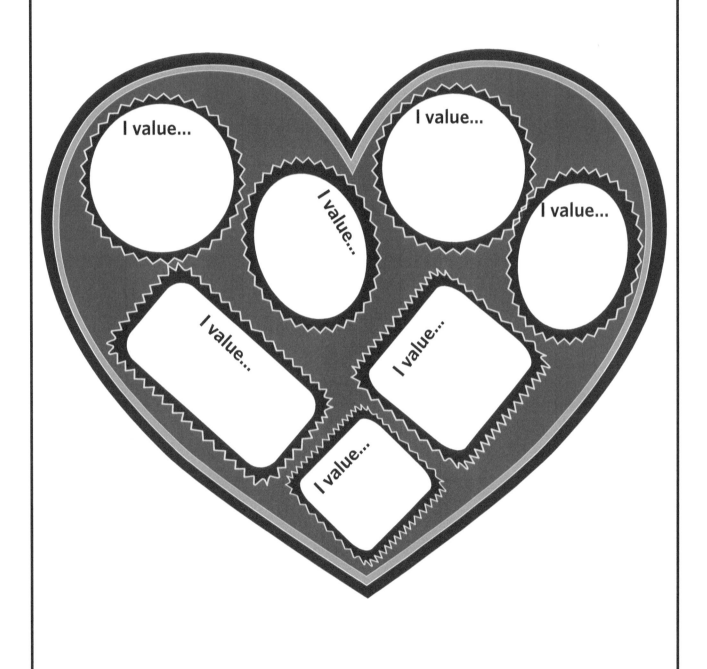

3.17 "WITH ME" WATER BOTTLES

DESCRIPTION:

Children with separation anxiety benefit from external focal points that can induce the regulation response. When these are paired with anchors to the caregiver, their regulating effects are amplified. This soothing bottle incorporates a small personal item (such as a key, necklace, or ring) that belongs to the caregiver to help soothe the child while helping them feel connected to the caregiver.

TREATMENT GOALS:

- Offer a transitional object from the absent caregiver to the current moment
- Create an external focal point in a soothing bottle that can be used during naptimes and at bedtime when the client is separated from the caregiver

MATERIALS NEEDED:

- Glass or plastic bottle or jar
- Food coloring
- Corn syrup or glycerin
- Hot glue gun or another adhesive
- Sequins, glitter, or other decorations
- A personal item offered by the caregiver

DIRECTIONS:

1. Introduce the client to the materials. Explain that the moments when we slow down are the times when we are most likely to miss our attachment figures.

2. Have the caregiver and child create a With Me water bottle together:

    a. Pour corn syrup or glycerin into the bottle. Do not overfill—leave enough room for the personal item and decorations.

    b. Add the food coloring, sequins, glitter, and any other decorations into the liquid.

3. When the bottle is ready, drop in the personal item from the caregiver and seal the bottle by gluing it shut (a hot glue gun works best, but please take care in allowing it to cool before handling the bottle!).

4. Identify times when using the bottle might be really helpful, like at naptime, at bedtime, or on long car rides. Offer the bottle to the client and invite them to gently shake it, then watch the colors and shapes shift as they allow themselves to relax.

BEJEWELING AFFIRMATIONS

DESCRIPTION:

Children with big behaviors receive frequent corrections from their caregivers and teachers. The tension created in the caregiver-child relationship when a child is easily dysregulated requires more doses of nurturing, delighting-in communications between the caregiver and child to ensure that the relationship remains connected and nurturing. This intervention offers a playful path to enhancing affirmations between the caregiver and child.

TREATMENT GOALS:

- Enhance the attachment relationship between the caregiver and child through words of affirmation, nurturing touch, and loving eye gaze

MATERIALS NEEDED:

- A variety of stickers or jewels

DIRECTIONS:

1. Invite the caregiver and child into a "nurture nook," a boundaried area defined by a rug, a large sittable pillow, or a snuggly, oversized chair.

2. Introduce a variety of stickers to choose from. Some children prefer sparkly gems with sticky backing, others prefer hearts, and still others prefer basketballs or emoji stickers. Offering the variety encourages choice and shared power in the dyad.

3. Model for the dyad how the activity works, starting with the caregiver. Verbalize one positive affirmation to the caregiver (e.g., "I love to hear your laugh—it is so genuine!") and then ask the caregiver where, on their body, they would like to place the sticker. Repeat this process with the child, sharing an affirmation and asking where the child would like the sticker on their body. By asking this, the therapist models body autonomy, which can be especially important for children who have had any sort of body boundary violation. Be sure to model various forms of affirmation. Emphasize your clients' competencies, resiliencies, and connecting characteristics (e.g., kindness, thoughtfulness, creativity, courage) rather than their physical features.

4. Invite the caregiver to share an affirmation and a sticker with their child, then invite the child to affirm and bejewel their caregiver in return. Repeat the process as many times as the dyad would like.

VARIATION:

An alternative approach is to first delight in the caregiver and child *together*—for example, "You both have such beautiful brown eyes!" Then ask them to decide together where each of their jewels or stickers will go.

3.19 I'M A ROBOT*

DESCRIPTION:

Children with big behaviors can get mired in patterns of noncompliance and defiance. This intervention encourages children to follow directions in a playful way and requires trust in the caregiver to give Safe Boss directions. In the game, the child is a robot, and the safe adult is the robot controller. The robot can only move if the controller tells it to, and only with touch. When working on attachment, it is a fun and safe way to incorporate healthy touch. When working on strengthening the client's sense of safety with adults, it puts the adult in the "in-charge" role and allows the child to see the benefit of trusting them. It makes the practice of concentrating, listening, and following directives into a fun game.

TREATMENT GOALS:

- Increase nurturing interactions between the caregiver and child
- Provide multiple opportunities for the client to succeed in following directions
- Enhance trust between the caregiver and child

MATERIALS NEEDED:

- None

DIRECTIONS:

1. Set up simple instructions (e.g., a tap on the head means take a step, two taps means take two steps, a squeeze of the shoulder means turn, a squeeze of the hand means pick something up). Create the instructions based on the client's developmental level.

2. Give the child a task (e.g., walk across the room and pick up the stuffed animal), and have the adult use the appropriate touch signals to move the child toward the goal.

3. You should both encourage their progress and be the one to send them backward if a rule is broken (so that the adult is not the "bad guy" for attachment purposes, and the focus can be on the two working together).

VARIATIONS:

- For older youth, make the directions complicated.
- For all ages, you can add a "prize" element to the game by making the end goal something like picking up a treat for everyone.
- If the sole use of the game is for attachment purposes, the child and adult can switch roles to allow the child to both accept and give healthy touch.

*Created by Michelle Codington, MS, LMFT, RPT-S, CFPT.

3.20 HEARTFELT FOLLOW-THE-LEADER*

DESCRIPTION:

Clients with big behaviors often need shared power in the family system. This activity can help dyads and families practice attunement, while giving each family member (including the child) the opportunity to be in control.

TREATMENT GOALS:

- Increase attunement
- Enhance family connections
- Teach turn-taking

MATERIALS NEEDED:

- Modeling clay

DIRECTIONS:

1. Give everyone the same amount of modeling clay. Tell one family member to start molding the clay, and tell the other family members to follow their lead. This might involve rolling the modeling clay in their hands, pounding it on the table, and so forth.

2. Have them take turns by calling out "switch" so that another person takes the lead. Each transition should flow into the next, like a dance. They are mirroring one another throughout the activity.

3. After everyone has had a turn, instruct them to roll the modeling clay in their hands to create a long piece (like a snake). This left- and right-hand movement also helps to activate the left and right hemispheres of the brain to raise alertness and "wake up the brain."

4. Once they all have their long pieces of modeling clay, have them create a large heart together to celebrate their love and strength as a family.

VARIATIONS:

The clients can write down some of the strengths of their family and what they love most about one another, then place these inside the heart. They can also make little balls out of additional modeling clay to symbolize the different strengths in the family (e.g., loving, strong, kind, creative, resilient) and place each ball in the heart.

---

*Created by Tammi Van Hollander, LCSW, RPT-S.

four

Understanding Our Stress Responses

Many clinicians are familiar with the triune brain model, which provides an evolutionary understanding of brain development in humans (MacLean, 1990). According to the model, the human brain can be divided into three regions that developed in a hierarchical manner. The first to develop was the reptilian brain, which consists of the brainstem and cerebellum and is tasked with basic survival functions, like heart rate and breathing. The next to develop was the limbic system, including the amygdala and hippocampus, which governs emotions and the stress response. Finally, the most recent area to develop was the neocortex, which governs higher-order thinking. Although the triune brain model has recently been debunked in the scientific community for being overly simplistic, it continues to provide caregivers and children with a helpful introduction to bottom-up brain development.

Children with big behaviors often need to have their lower brain regions regulated first, and they need to feel connected to others before any real cognitive absorption can occur. The brainstem is always asking, "Am I safe?" whereas the limbic system is always asking, "Am I loved?"—and both of these questions need to be answered with a resounding *yes* before the neocortex can ask, "What can I learn from this?" (Bailey, 2004). These concepts, while admittedly oversimplistic, offer a paradigm shift that helps reopen the well of compassion among exhausted parents, teachers, and others. In addition, TraumaPlay therapists offer psychoeducational nuggets regarding bottom-up development (Perry, 2009) in developmentally sensitive ways. For example, the amygdala becomes Amy G. Dala as a way to externalize this brain structure.

Also included in this chapter are activities based on polyvagal theory (Porges, 2011), which has given us a whole new way of understanding the autonomic nervous system. We have long been aware that our nervous system is composed of a sympathetic nervous system (fight-or-flight response) and a parasympathetic nervous system (shut-down response). Until recently, we thought these two systems operated in antagonistic fashion, warring with each other in our bodies for dominance. However, polyvagal theory has shed light on a third system known as the ventral vagal system, which is also governed by the parasympathetic nervous system. To understand this better, it is important to realize that the vagus nerve consists of two different branches, both of which move us into parasympathetic dominance. Whereas the dorsal vagal branch of the parasympathetic nervous system becomes activated under conditions of life threat (causing us to immobilize and shut down), the ventral vagal branch becomes activated under the neuroception of safety (causing us to move into connection with others). It is for this reason that the ventral vagal branch is often called the *social engagement system*. Therefore, this chapter also offers several interventions that provide playful, child-friendly opportunities for children to reflect on their own neuroception of safety.

Finally, many children with big behaviors have a narrowed window of tolerance for distress. When they become overly stressed, they may kick into a state of hyperarousal in which the sympathetic nervous system is in charge, causing racing thoughts, rage, irritability, inattention, impulsivity, or hyperkinetic movement. Alternatively, they may kick down into a state of hypoarousal, where the parasympathetic nervous system slows the body and mind down, resulting in fuzzy cognitions, withdrawal, fatigue, numbing, and dissociation. Helping clients and their caregivers become more aware of their windows of tolerance—and learning ways to stretch their window or to more quickly come back into a state of optimal arousal—can be important in the change process. Therefore, additional play therapy interventions are provided to help children name the arousal states that accompany the unique wiring of their autonomic nervous system. Because the arousal states of children are often tied to the arousal states of their caregivers, this concept is valuable when offering psychoeducation and building reflective capacity with caregivers, teachers, teens, and children—and with the therapists and counselors who help them.

Note: Children benefit from having concepts introduced in a step-wise fashion, where each concept builds on the one before it. We begin with helping children understand the window of tolerance (WOT) more deeply. Then we help them personalize their WOT. The next set of activities introduces the amygdala in a playful way. Finally, the remaining activities in this chapter help children understand polyvagal theory and our stress-response systems through relatable characters and metaphors.

4.1 WOT ARE YOU?

DESCRIPTION:

Children with big behaviors need psychoeducation about the window of tolerance (WOT) in order to begin reflecting on how they get kicked out of their optimal arousal zone. Sometimes, children with big behaviors also have caregivers with big behaviors or big emotions. This exercise is simply meant to provide a cross-hemispheric structure for children to reflect on their WOT, as well as for caregivers to identify whether they tend to kick up into hyperarousal or down into hypoarousal when they are stressed.

TREATMENT GOALS:

- Provide developmentally sensitive psychoeducation about the window of tolerance

- Access left- and right-brain ways of knowing by creating symbols for the different states of arousal

MATERIALS NEEDED:

- *WOT Are You?* handout

- Modeling clay

- Markers

DIRECTIONS:

1. Explain to the client and their caregiver that you are going to be learning about the window of tolerance today. (For younger kids, I like to say it in a loud, drawn-out voice to be more dramatic: "WIIIIINDOW OF TOOOOOLERANCE!!!") Introduce the window of tolerance in this way:

   "Our bodies respond to stress in some really interesting ways. When we feel 'just right,' we're in what's called our *optimal arousal zone*. Imagine a baby who has eaten, has slept, and is now snuggling with their mom. That baby feels content and relaxed. This is the optimal zone to be in, meaning it's the best! But when that baby gets hungry or feels scared or hurt, they may begin to scream, cry, and tense their body. The baby has now been kicked into a state of *hyperarousal*. Finally, when the baby is tired, they may get groggy, zone out, and even fall asleep. That baby is now in a state of *hypoarousal*."

2. When explaining the window of tolerance, let the child know that all kids are different: Some mostly go into the zone of hypoarousal, which means they shut down, become numb, feel sad, or freeze. Other kids go into the zone of hyperarousal by yelling, hitting, running, or fighting. Make sure the child and caregiver understand that every person has a unique window.

3. Invite the client and their caregiver to create a symbol out of modeling clay (or markers) to represent themselves in their optimal arousal zone, and place it in the middle column of the paper. Repeat this prompt for hyperarousal and hypoarousal.

4. This symbolic exercise can be useful with children, teens, caregivers, and even teachers. After all symbols have been created, ask the client to share about what they made.

5. Then ask the follow-up question: "What do you need to stay inside your optimal arousal zone more often, or to come back into it more quickly when you are stressed?"

WOT ARE YOU? HANDOUT

Create a symbol with clay or markers to represent yourself in each of these states.

OVERRESPONDING	BEST SELF	UNDERRESPONDING
Hyperarousal	Optimal Arousal	Hypoarousal

4.2 | MY BRAIN AND MY WINDOW*

DESCRIPTION:

This intervention provides a developmentally sensitive way to explain clients' stress-response systems. Each part of the triune brain is described in child-friendly language, and a developmentally sensitive way to explain how we come in and out of our optimal arousal zone is offered.

TREATMENT GOALS:

- Provide an understanding of the triune brain
- Teach the child to manage emotion dysregulation
- Teach the caregivers to help their child organize their feelings

MATERIALS NEEDED:

- *My Brain and My Window* information sheet

DIRECTIONS:

1. After you have introduced the concept of the window of tolerance using the *WOT Are You?* activity (4.1), tell the child and caregiver that today they will be learning about the different parts of the brain.

2. Explain the following:

   "Your brain works like a high-powered computer, with many different programs working at the same time! The brain has three main parts working together: the neocortex (or thinking brain), the limbic brain (or bear brain), and the reptilian brain (or dinosaur brain). When they are all working together, you feel safe, and you are able to think before you act and make decisions calmly without feeling overwhelmed or withdrawn."

3. Go over the *My Brain and My Window* information sheet to further explain the thinking, bear, and dinosaur brains, and demonstrate how the body feels when all the parts of the brain are working together as a team.

4. Discuss how these different brain regions operate in relation to the window of tolerance. Explain that when some kids get stressed or scared, they jump out of their window of tolerance into one of the other two zones, which means they can become anxious or overwhelmed and respond by fighting, by running, or in lots of other ways: "When you get really scared, stressed, or overwhelmed—and all the parts of your brain are not working together—you can leave your window of tolerance, and your bear and dinosaur brains take control!"

---

*Created by Lindsey Townsend, LCSW, and Tasha Jackson, LCSW.

MY BRAIN AND MY WINDOW INFORMATION SHEET

The Reptilian Brain (Dinosaur Brain)

The first part of your brain to develop was your reptilian brain, but we will call it the dinosaur brain. It is located in the back of your head and is programmed to automatically help you survive. The dinosaur brain controls your heart rate, breathing, body temperature, and balance.

Dinosaurs had tiny brains, and they could not think or plan well. Dinosaurs had to be BIG and powerful, or be able to run away FAST, to protect themselves from danger. Even today, when you feel threatened and your dinosaur brain becomes active, you will automatically go into fight, flight, or freeze mode.

The Limbic Brain (Teddy Bear Brain)

The second part of your brain that developed was your limbic brain, but we will call it the teddy bear brain. This part of your brain, which controls your emotions, is located deep in the center of your brain, behind your eyes. The teddy bear brain records your memories—it remembers the good and bad stuff.

A big part of your teddy bear brain's job is to make sense of your experiences so you know how to respond. This part of your brain can be happy, grumpy, sad, or any other emotion.

The Neocortex (Thinking Brain)

The biggest and last part of your brain is the neocortex, but we will call it the thinking brain. It is located behind your forehead and is the outside, top layer of the brain. Your thinking brain is the part of your brain that thinks logically and creatively and makes you human. It allows you to be imaginative and inventive. It likes to solve problems, enjoys learning new things, and helps you communicate your ideas.

The Optimal Zone

When all parts of your brain are working together, the thoughts flow freely between all three parts of your brain—back to front, bottom to top, and side to side. Your body responds by feeling light, good, and relaxed. You are in your window of tolerance, which is the zone where you feel calm and can think through how to best solve problems.

Leaving Your Window of Tolerance

When you feel threatened or scared, the dinosaur brain and teddy bear brain react quickly to protect you, which prevents you from using your thinking brain. You leave your window of tolerance and go into survival mode! Your teddy bear brain feels fear, and your dinosaur brain wants to fight, run away, or freeze.

4.3 MAKING MY WINDOW

DESCRIPTION:

This intervention provides a developmentally sensitive way to explain clients' stress-response systems, giving particular attention to helping the client recognize what sorts of situations can kick them out of their window of tolerance.

TREATMENT GOALS:

- Provide an understanding of the window of tolerance
- Teach the child to manage emotion dysregulation
- Help the child and caregiver recognize and communicate when the child is beginning to leave their window of tolerance

MATERIALS NEEDED:

- Construction paper in black, green, red, and blue
- Glue
- Scissors
- Markers or pens

DIRECTIONS:

1. Take a piece of black construction paper to serve as the background and three pieces of colored paper to serve as the different zones of arousal (i.e., hypoarousal, hyperarousal, and optimal zone within the window of tolerance).

2. Help the child determine the size that each zone should be and cut the colored paper accordingly: green (optimal) in the middle, red (hyperarousal) on the left, and blue (hypoarousal) on the right.

3. Have the child glue each panel to the black construction paper. The entire paper should be covered to create a three-pane window.

4. While working on each zone, invite the child to draw symbols of what it feels like to be in and out of their window of tolerance. For example, the child might feel super excited when they move toward the hyperarousal zone, but this excitement may turn to anxiety or fear if they leave their window of tolerance. Help the child recognize their warning signs, and invite the caregiver to participate in the detective work.

5. The caregiver and child should work together as a team of window detectives, learning to manage the child's big feelings before they move out of their window and creating a regulation action plan. The caregiver might identify what the child can do whenever they notice that their heart is beginning to race, such as taking three deep, diaphragmatic breaths.

6. The child and caregiver should be encouraged to use the language of "being out of my window" to communicate the presence of big feelings and the need for a co-regulator.

4.4 | WHO IS AMY G. DALA?

DESCRIPTION:

Clients with big behaviors benefit from understanding their neural architecture, including how the amygdala responds when danger cues are present. The client can't see their own amygdala, so it can be helpful to create an external representation that they can play with and to give it a voice. This externalization can decrease the client's sense of shame around their stress reactions. After completing this activity, you can further build upon the concepts using *What Is Amy G. Saying Now?* (activity 4.5) and then *Soothing Amy G.* (activity 4.6).

TREATMENT GOALS:

- Provide developmentally sensitive psychoeducation about the stress response
- Offer a sense of empowerment in relation to the amygdala alarm by externalizing it

MATERIALS NEEDED:

- Tissue paper
- Duct tape
- Permanent markers (in multiple colors, if possible)

DIRECTIONS:

1. Introduce the amygdala to the client using Siegel's (2010) hand brain model. To explain this model, put your thumb in the middle of your hand to represent the amygdala and explain the following:

   "The amygdala is an almond-shaped cluster of cells in the middle of your brain. When we hear, see, smell, taste, or touch something that might be dangerous for us, the amygdala reacts right away to keep us safe. We might yank our hand off a hot surface, spit out some yucky-tasting rotten tomato, or run away from a loud sound. Each of these things happens before we really have time to think about it."

2. Acknowledge that *amygdala* is a pretty weird word and can be hard to remember, so you two will create an almond-shaped person, named Amy G. Dala, to help you remember.

3. Using tissue paper and duct tape, create an almond-shaped body, then use permanent markers to personalize your version of Amy together. You can draw on long eyelashes, red lips, a buzz cut, glasses, or any other features you like.

AMY G. DALA

4.5 | WHAT IS AMY G. SAYING NOW?

DESCRIPTION:

Once you have created a personified version of the amygdala and given her the name Amy G. Dala (using the *Who Is Amy G. Dala?* activity [4.4]), use this intervention to help clients identify the triggers that activate the stress response and kick them out of their optimal arousal zone. After completing this activity, you can further build upon the concepts using *Soothing Amy G.* (activity 4.6).

TREATMENT GOALS:

- Provide developmentally sensitive psychoeducation about the stress response
- Offer a sense of empowerment in relation to the amygdala alarm by externalizing it

MATERIALS NEEDED:

- Amy G. Dala prop (made previously by the client)
- *What Is Amy G. Saying Now?* handout
- Permanent marker

DIRECTIONS:

1. Review Siegel's (2010) hand brain model and remind the client that the amygdala reacts immediately, bypassing our thinking brain to get us out of the way of danger.

2. Invite the client to make an even larger mouth on Amy G. because she often blurts things out and yells at the body to "do something, quick!"

3. Using the *What Is Amy G. Saying Now?* handout, have the client fill in words to represent the things Amy G. might yell. For example, if the client has experienced trauma related to someone hurting their body, when someone gets in their physical space, Amy G. might yell, "Hit them! Push them! Get them out of your space!" This may result in the client becoming physically aggressive toward a peer who gets too close to them before they have time to think through another response, like using their words.

4. Help the client connect the bossy words Amy G. says to their resulting actions. For example, if the client feels inadequate when doing math, Amy G. might say, "Get out of there!" resulting in the client running out of the classroom when the math gets too hard. This process of becoming curious about what Amy G. says is the first step in helping clients figure out how to soothe or reassure Amy G.

5. If the client has trouble getting started, use a recent upsetting moment that resulted in big behavior of some kind and work backward from there to what Amy G. was saying.

WHAT IS AMY G. SAYING NOW? HANDOUT

In the spaces below, fill in all the things Amy G. might yell at you when she senses danger!

AMY G. DALA

4.6 SOOTHING AMY G.

DESCRIPTION:

This intervention should be used after you have completed the two previous activities— *Who Is Amy G. Dala?* (4.4) and *What Is Amy G. Saying Now?* (4.5)—in which you personified the amygdala and helped your client identify their stress-response triggers. This intervention helps the client come up with and practice adaptive self-talk that can mitigate the stress response.

TREATMENT GOALS:

- Provide psychoeducation about the stress response
- Identify adaptive self-talk that mitigates the stress response
- Rehearse adaptive self-talk statements while experiencing the insulating effect of cognitive replacement work through kinesthetic involvement

MATERIALS NEEDED:

- Amy G. Dala prop (made previously by the client)
- Completed *What Is Amy G. Saying Now?* handout
- Soft materials such as paper towels, facial tissue, cotton balls, and fabric

DIRECTIONS:

1. Review Siegel's (2010) hand brain model again, reminding the client that the amygdala reacts immediately, bypassing our thinking brain to get us out of the way of danger.

2. Review the completed *What Is Amy G. Saying Now?* handout with the client, and explore together what Amy G. might need to feel better in each of those situations. She might need education—for example, "When your classmate came close to you, Amy G. screamed, 'Hit him! Make him back off!' But she just needed to be told, 'Actually, that classmate is just walking by to get to the water fountain. You are still safe.'" You can even have the client thank Amy G. for doing her job and then practice soothing or reassuring her.

3. For two to three weeks after the introduction of these concepts, apply this sequence of questions to moments when big behaviors happen:

   a. What is Amy G. saying right now? What information is she missing?

   b. How can you reassure her? What can you teach her?

4. The soft materials can be used to make a bed, blanket, pillow, or lovie for Amy G., helping her to feel soothed and safe. Some of the reassuring statements can be written on these objects—for example, "It's okay for kids to come close to you now. You are safe in the classroom."

EMBEDDING AMY G.

DESCRIPTION:

When helping children better understand their stress-response systems, concretely placing an amygdala "stand-in" inside a plush brain can help in the psychoeducation process. This intervention should be used after *What Is Amy G. Saying Now?* (activity 4.5) to help the client understand that stress-response systems look different in different creatures.

TREATMENT GOALS:

- Provide psychoeducation about the stress response
- Identify and practice adaptive self-talk that mitigates the stress response

MATERIALS NEEDED:

- Almonds*
- Stuffed animals
- Scissors
- Tweezers
- Needle and thread

DIRECTIONS:

1. Ask the family to bring in a stuffed animal from home that they wouldn't mind being cut and sewn, or provide stuffed animals for the client to choose from.

2. Remind the client about Amy G. Dala—the almond-shaped cluster of cells in the midbrain that helps to raise the alarm when we are afraid or stressed.

3. Turn your attention to the stuffed animal. Invite the client to decide which stress response the stuffed animal may have: fight, flight, or freeze. Then allow them to cut a hole in the midbrain, insert an actual almond, and sew it back up (with your help and supervision, of course!).

4. Explore what the Amy G. Dala inside that stuffed animal says when she's alarmed and what she needs to be reassured that she is actually okay, even when she feels that she is not safe: "When she starts to yell 'Freeze!' 'Run away as quick as you can!' or 'Play dead!' she may need you to tell her that you've got her, that she's okay."

5. Young clients are especially helped by seeing the amygdala concretely represented by the almond. The psychoeducation around this brain structure is further helped by kinesthetically placing the symbol inside the stuffed animal.

6. Role-play a variety of scenarios in which the stuffed animal might feel stressed, and work with the client to provide adaptive coping responses to disarm the amygdala.

---

*Check with the caregiver in advance to ensure there are no food allergies to almonds. If so, you can make pretend almonds out of modeling clay.

4.8 MARACA MADNESS

DESCRIPTION:

When a child or teen client is engaged in a big behavior like screaming, kicking, hitting, or running away, their sympathetic nervous system is activated. In these moments, the child needs a caregiver to co-regulate them. However, caregivers may want to reason with their child during times of upset, using lots of words to try to calm them, further stimulating the child. This activity is geared toward helping caregivers and children alike better understand how the stress response is experienced during escalated moments.

TREATMENT GOALS:

- Explain sympathetic nervous system response patterns
- Offer a metaphor for how escalation limits our ability to take in new information
- Give permission for quiet co-regulation by caregivers

MATERIALS NEEDED:

- Four plastic spoons
- Two empty plastic eggs
- Small, hard items such as dry beans, uncooked rice, beads, or LEGO® bricks
- Decorative tape
- String
- Stick-on jewels or other decorations

DIRECTIONS:

1. Explain that you will be making maracas to represent all the "noise" that is in our brains when we are upset.

2. Open the plastic eggs and invite the client to put in one bean/item for each of their current stressors. Close the eggs and shake them. Explain that as stress builds, it can feel like louder and louder noise in our brains, and this makes it difficult to take in new information or really hear what other people are saying.

3. Tape each egg between two plastic spoons. Wrap tape around the maracas until they are completely covered, then invite the child and caregiver to decorate them.

4. Have the child and caregiver keep the maracas close to their laps and shake them while you talk for twenty seconds about why you like apples. Then have the child and caregiver hold the maracas right by their ears and shake them vigorously while you tell them why you like bananas. Ask if they could hear you talking about why you like bananas.

5. Explain that the difficulty they had hearing you when the maracas were shaking by their ears is the same difficulty they will encounter when the child is having a tantrum or raging. Word-based strategies are unlikely to be effective. Instead, it is most helpful to co-regulate the child by using a soft tone of voice and a friendly face, by using touch and physical proximity, and by providing a grounded presence in a contained environment (Goodyear-Brown, 2010a, 2021).

4.9 BALANCING ON THE HEAD OF A PIN

DESCRIPTION:

Children with big behaviors often have neurophysiological sensitivities that make it difficult for them to distinguish between excitement and anxiety. Even really fun events can lead to meltdowns or tantrums simply because the stress response tips over from excitation into anxiety or aggression. This graphical representation can support caregivers in shifting the meaning they assign to big behaviors away from the misconception that the child is "choosing" misbehavior and toward an understanding that the child is outside of their window of tolerance for stress.

TREATMENT GOALS:

- Explain sympathetic nervous system response patterns
- Offer a metaphor for how escalation limits our ability to take in new information
- Give permission for quiet co-regulation by caregivers

MATERIALS NEEDED:

- Pushpins
- A pin cushion
- *Head of a Pin* handout

DIRECTIONS:

1. Explain the different sympathetic nervous system response patterns to the caregiver and child using the following script:

   "Some stress is good for us. Good stress might even be called *excitement*. Imagine that you are standing in line for a big roller-coaster. You are nervous and excited. It can be hard to tell where the excitement ends and where the nervousness begins. That's because they balance on the head of a pin inside your brain. To complicate things even more, when we get over-excited or over-anxious, we can get kicked out of our window of tolerance for stress of any kind, and we can become aggressive—yelling, screaming, or even hitting. We are usually not in control of our stress response at those moments."

2. Show the client a pushpin and insert it in the pin cushion while explaining the following:

   "Imagine a tiny pin inside your brain. All three experiences—anxiety, aggression, and excitement—are constantly balancing on the head of this pin. And when we have too much (even of a good thing), it can be too much for us. Can you remember a time when you were excited or having fun and then everything fell apart?"

3. If the client has trouble generating situations, you can offer some:

    a. You are so excited to go to the trampoline park, but after seeing all the lights and all the noise—and having several fun jumps—your fuse gets shorter.

    b. You are so excited to play a video game with friends, and you are really into it, but you lose the round (or your friends don't follow your lead the way you'd like them to), and you lose your temper. You move from excitement to aggression faster than your brain can keep up.

4. Using the *Head of a Pin* handout, label the three images: excitement, anxiety, and aggression.

5. Invite the caregiver and child to each generate scenarios that can start out fun and then become too much.

6. Work with the caregiver on consciously keeping the client within their window of tolerance for excitation.

HEAD OF A PIN HANDOUT

On the lines below, write down whether the image represents excitement, anxiety, or aggression. Then think of examples that start out as fun but quickly become too much.

Balancing on the head of a pin...

_____   _____   _____

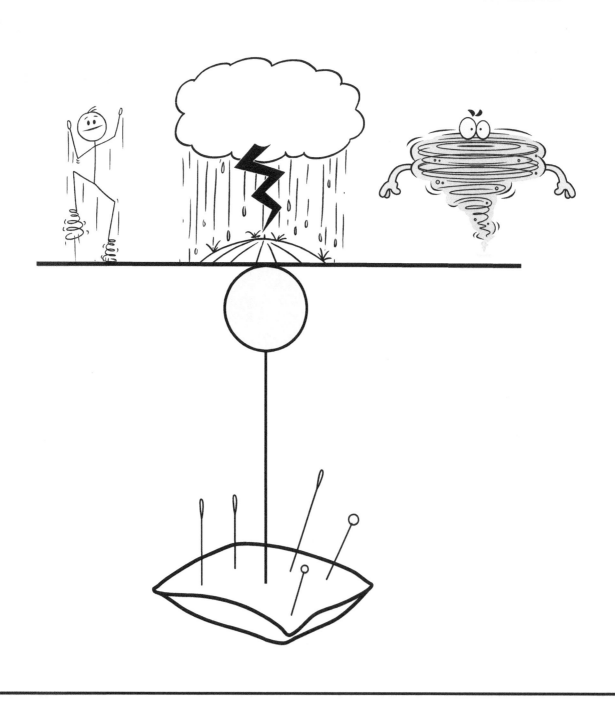

DESCRIPTION:

This intervention offers a way to frame the stress-response states explained in Stephen Porges's polyvagal theory in terms that children and their caregivers can easily understand. States of mobilization, immobilization, and social engagement are each represented with different animals. These animals, and their stress responses, can serve as shorthand within family systems for our more complex sympathetic and parasympathetic (dorsal and ventral vagal) response patterns.

TREATMENT GOALS:

- Explain polyvagal theory in developmentally sensitive terms
- Pair the polyvagal states with animals that represent different stress-response patterns

MATERIALS NEEDED:

- *Polyvagal Zoo* handout
- Sand tray
- Miniature versions of a sloth, a goat, a bear, a roadrunner, and two monkeys

DIRECTIONS:

1. Introduce the first animal in the Polyvagal Zoo—the fainting goat—to the client or family (see Goodyear-Brown, 2021) using the following script:

   "There is this really cool nerve in our bodies called the *vagus nerve*, which attaches at the base of your brain and runs all the way down into your gut. The vagus nerve helps us decide how best to respond to danger in various situations—and our reaction patterns go all the way back to when dinosaurs roamed the earth. If a little creature was about to be eaten by a dinosaur, it would play dead. Since most big, meat-eating predators liked their meat fresh (alive!), they might lose interest in an animal that is already dead. In our Polyvagal Zoo, we represent this death-feigning response with a fainting goat. Have you ever seen a fainting goat? They are hilarious. Whenever their nervous systems get excited, their whole bodies freeze up and they fall over, with their legs sticking straight up in the air. After about 30 seconds or so, their bodies relax and they go about their business. It doesn't matter whether they are excited because it's dinnertime or they're scared of a predator— their bodies freeze up just the same. The fainting goat represents our dorsal vagal freeze response, and we call this *Dying Very Suddenly*."

Continue introducing the various animals using the following scripts:

a. **The Sloth:** "This freeze response can also show up much more quietly, creating a feeling of numbness over time. When we have small threats to our self-esteem (like studying really hard for a test and still failing, or being bullied day in and day out at school) our sense of being able to do hard things gets scraped away, bit by bit. We call this pattern *Dying Very Slowly*, and we use the sloth to represent this state."

b. **The Roadrunner and the Bear:** "When you feel like you don't have any choices, you might freeze like the fainting goat. But when you see danger coming and still have enough time to make a choice, you might decide to fight back (like the bear in the picture, who is being attacked by angry hornets) or run away (like the roadrunner). We call this our fight-or-flight response."

c. **The Monkeys:** "When our minds and bodies are feeling safe, our social engagement system is active. We can play, learn, and work with our friends, our siblings, and our Safe Bosses to stay connected, ask for what we need kindly and calmly, and stick together with others. We call this pattern *Very Very Social* and use a pair of monkeys to represent it."

2. Once all the animals have been described, you can create the zoo can using the sand tray, with enclosures designed for each animal. Explore with the client the animals that seem the most aligned with how they respond to stress.

3. It can also be helpful to bring caregivers into this exploration. You can engage in a follow-up conversation with the caregiver that explores how other people help the child feel safe versus unsafe. As caregivers become curious about how the child perceives their tone of voice and face in different situations, it can begin to shift them toward more social engagement.

99

4.11 SLEUTH THE SLOTH

DESCRIPTION:

When big behaviors occur, it may be that the client's window of tolerance for distress or excitation is too narrow. This results in the client shifting quickly into hyperarousal or hypoarousal when they are confronted with a stressful situation. Thinking about behavior through a polyvagal lens, the dorsal vagal response can present as an immediate freeze response or a slowing response. In TraumaPlay, we use a sloth to represent the dorsal vagal response.

TREATMENT GOALS:

- Teach a dorsal vagal response that involves a slowing of our responses
- Normalize the hypoarousal response, window of tolerance, and polyvagal immobilization
- Identify safety signals the client might need to get back into their optimal arousal zone

MATERIALS NEEDED:

- Stuffed sloth
- *Zootopia*™ (2016 Disney film)
- Essential oils*
- Small pieces of fabric
- Permanent marker

DIRECTIONS:

1. Invite the client to hold the stuffed sloth while viewing the short scene from *Zootopia* with the sloth in the Department of Motor Vehicles. (The therapist can cue up the part of the movie beforehand or search for the specific scene on YouTube.)

2. Ask the client about slowed responses, or times that they feel "fuzzy" in their brains—when it is difficult to make decisions or to feel motivated to do chores, homework, or exercise.

3. Trace the sloth's paw on a piece of fabric and write adaptive strategies for upregulating their bodies on or around the fabric paw. This should include things that will help the client move forward and do hard things when they are feeling slowed or fuzzy. Examples of adaptive coping might include playing upbeat music, taking an energizing shower, eating something crunchy or cold, or jogging around the block.

4. Offer a variety of essential oils that would counter the slowing response, including peppermint, vetiver, lemongrass, wild citrus, eucalyptus, and bergamot. Allow the client to explore the oils and choose one that helps them feel alert. Have them put drops of this oil on the fabric paw.

5. Have them take the fabric home, and when they begin to feel most sloth-like, encourage them to sniff the fabric of the sloth paw and use their adaptive strategies.

---

*Check for allergies before using any essential oils.

4.12 | FARMERS AND THE FAINTING GOAT

DESCRIPTION:

The fainting goat is a unique breed of goat that has an autonomic nervous system that responds to sudden excitation *of any kind* with a freeze response. The goats become rigid and fall over, usually rolling onto their backs with their legs rising straight into the air. While this causes no permanent damage, it is frustrating to have such a hair-trigger stress response. In TraumaPlay, we talk often about how excitement, aggression, and anxiety balance on the head of a pin neurophysiologically for traumatized children. The fainting goat offers a fun and accessible metaphor for the child's own response.

TREATMENT GOALS:

- Explain the reactivity of the stress-response system, specifically "freeze," in a playful way

- Articulate ways to mitigate the excitation of the stress-response system

- Apply this mitigation to the client's systems, including home and school

MATERIALS NEEDED:

- YouTube videos of fainting goats exhibiting the freeze response

DIRECTIONS:

1. Explain Porges's polyvagal theory in developmentally sensitive terms:

   "Earlier, we learned about the ways our bodies react when we are really stressed or scared. We learned that we might fight like an angry bear or run away like a roadrunner. But when the threat is so big and scary that we feel trapped—like there is no way out—we also learned that our bodies can freeze like a fainting goat. Today we're going to see what a fainting goat might need to avoid freezing up."

2. Offer the fainting goat videos as one example of how the freeze response can become activated when the neuroception of life threat is present. Explain how the body can become wired to automatically move into an immobilization response (even when there is no actual danger) when someone has endured trauma:

   "Thousands of years ago, when a smaller animal would get trapped by a meat-eating dinosaur, the animal's best hope of survival was to play dead. Dinosaurs like their meat fresh, so if the dinosaur thought the animal had been dead for a while, they would lose interest and move on. For you, when the scary thing happened [*insert language here as appropriate regarding physical abuse, sexual abuse, domestic violence, etc.*], you had no way out, so your body wisely chose to freeze. It was

101

your best way to survive. And the more times that scary thing happened, the more hardwired this response became. So now it is kind of like a habit for you to freeze when you feel stressed."

3. Identify what the farmer might say or do to help the fainting goats remain more regulated and faint less frequently. These strategies might include sidling up beside them instead of approaching them head-on or using a soft tone of voice and face.

4. Guide the client and their caregivers as they brainstorm things they currently do or say that might cause the freeze response, and then identify "fainting-goat-friendly" alternatives for each.

VARIATION:

For younger children, you can role-play these strategies in the sand tray with miniature goats or using animal hand puppets. The child can choose a predator figure/puppet, and the two of you can play through various scenarios.

five

Enhancing
Self-Regulation

Little ones learn to soothe themselves after being wholly soothed by their caregiver thousands and thousands of times. You've seen this cycle: The baby cries in distress, and the caregiver picks up the baby—rocking, murmuring, and soothing them—until the baby eventually sighs and collapses, molding into the warmth and softness of this caring other. An example of my daughter's developmental process can help explain the progression. Whenever she would cry in hunger or distress as a baby, I would nurse her until she was soothed. By the time she was six months old, she had learned to keep her hand on my clavicle and nurse whenever she was upset. By 13 months, she had stopped nursing but would suck her thumb and anchor her tiny hand to my collarbone. Six months after that, she no longer needed to touch me when she was distressed—she just sucked her thumb—and six months after that, she no longer needed to suck her thumb. Co-regulation by a caregiver always precedes self-regulation.

However, children who didn't get these repetitions of co-regulation due to neglect, maltreatment, or a multitude of other adverse childhood experiences never learn the ability to self-soothe, even in their later years. For example, a ten-year-old child who can get a perfect score on a math test when her neocortex is in charge may throw massive tantrums at home when she is stressed, making her present more like a two-year-old in terms of social-emotional development. Children with neurodivergent development may also have a hair-trigger amygdala alarm that kicks them out of their window of tolerance much more quickly than their peers. This lack of self-regulation sets them up for negative interactions with their classmates and caregivers that can ultimately damage their self-esteem.

Many children with big behaviors need help learning how to regulate themselves more quickly or more effectively. To do so, we want them to take advantage of all sorts of sensory-soothing experiences while also learning how to pay attention to their sense of interoception, or what their bodies are telling them. We frequently check in with clients about how hot or cold they are feeling, and we invite clients to use their words to ask for what they need. At Nurture House, you can hear clinicians saying, "Your body is letting me know…" or "What is your body telling you right now?" We design treatment areas to provide bigness and smallness in space, as some children can self-regulate more easily in snug spaces that offer a sense of safe containment, while others needed expansive space to move their bodies in the ways they need. In these spaces, we encourage clients to swing, jump, climb, spin, and run, offering regulation work through their proprioceptive and vestibular senses. Finally, we provide interventions that mobilize the five basic senses as a way of promoting regulation.

An important concept within the TraumaPlay model is that we are not working simply to calm the client, but to teach them to calm themselves. We help them to recognize more deeply when they are moving out of their optimal arousal zone and to determine the strategies that work best to help them return to this zone (i.e., to downregulate when they are in a state of hyperarousal or to upregulate when they are in a state of hypoarousal). The strategies in this chapter are all helpful in building skills for self-regulation for children with big behaviors.

5.1 PERSONALIZED PINWHEELS

DESCRIPTION:

Breath work can enhance regulation for clients who tend to escalate quickly when experiencing stress. However, when children have an autonomic nervous system response wired for hyperarousal due to trauma, asking the child to close their eyes and "relax" while breathing deeply may be perceived as dangerous. What they may see behind their closed eyelids is the trauma. Pairing breath work with an external focal point mitigates the client's hypervigilance while also increasing competency as they successfully spin the pinwheel.

TREATMENT GOALS:

- Help the client practice deep, diaphragmatic breathing
- Offer an external focal point to pair with deep breathing
- Increase the client's experience of competency in relaxation work

MATERIALS NEEDED:

- Make-your-own pinwheel kit, or the *Personalized Pinwheel* template and a straw or wooden dowel
- A premade pinwheel

DIRECTIONS:

1. Offer the premade pinwheel to the client for playtime in session.

2. Ask the client to hold the pinwheel very close to their mouth and to blow gently to make it spin. This will not be difficult for most children.

3. Now ask them to hold it as far away from their mouths as they can while still making it spin. This requires a deep inhalation and a focused exhalation of breath. For children who are easily distracted or who have experienced trauma and have trouble closing their eyes to relax, using the pinwheel as an external focal point can be therapeutically powerful.

4. Offer the kit or the template to the client and help them create their own pinwheel. They can decorate the pinwheel with mantras that are soothing to them or with stickers and drawings that help to ground them.

5. Their personalized pinwheel can go home with them, becoming a transitional object from the safety of the playroom and play therapist to their home environment.*

---

*If their anxiety is most intensely felt at bedtime, the client can be instructed to practice breathing while making the pinwheel spin for the first five minutes they are in bed. If a safe attachment figure can help with this breath work, that will aid in counterconditioning the child's body.

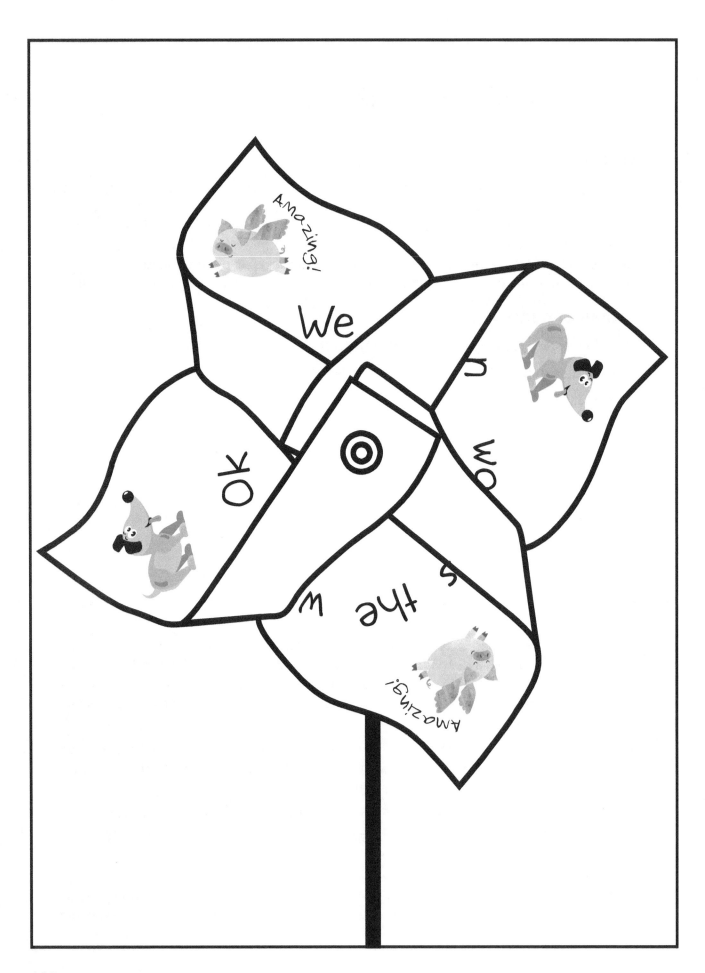

PERSONALIZED PINWHEEL TEMPLATE

Place a straw or wooden dowel through the hole in the center of the pinwheel. Starting with the top left-hand corner, pull that side into the middle and thread the hole onto the protruding dowel in the middle. Move clockwise from corner to corner, overlapping the next hole onto the dowel until all four edges are folded over and secured on the dowel.

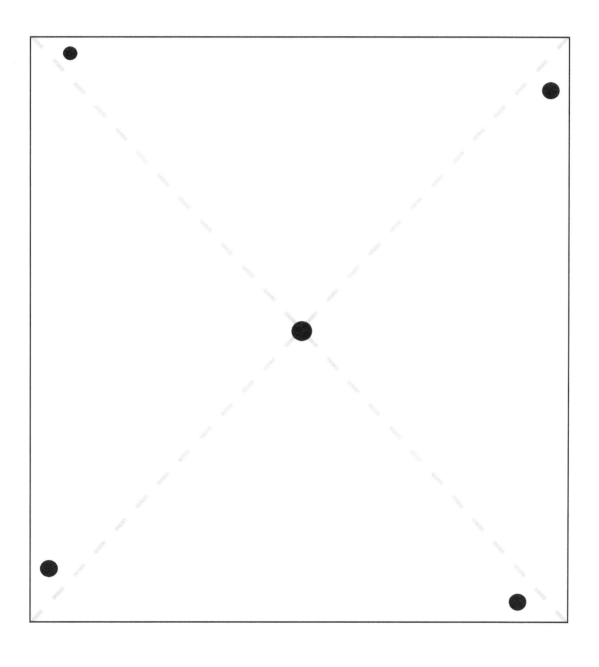

5.2 FIVE-COUNT BREATHING

DESCRIPTION:

Children with big behaviors move into states of hyperarousal more quickly than their peers. Rhythmic patterns of breathing in, holding their breath, and releasing their breath in a slow, controlled way can increase self-regulation and help bring escalated children back into balance. Traumatized children may find breath work scary, as the relaxation response and the decrease in vigilance may feel unsafe. Pairing the breath work with an external focal point (the paper) and a drawing task provides tactile grounding for the breathing exercise.

TREATMENT GOALS:

- Increase self-regulation through breath work
- Practice controlled, diaphragmatic breathing
- Mitigate the anxiety associated with a decrease in vigilance through a paired drawing task

MATERIALS NEEDED:

- *Five-Count Breathing* template
- One or more of the following:
  - Sheets of paper and markers
  - Dry-erase board and markers
  - Sand tray (or a pan and salt or sugar)

DIRECTIONS:

1. Draw a five-point star on a piece of paper. Give the client blank pieces of paper and invite tracing practice until they are comfortable with drawing the five-point star. Drawing a five-point star with their pointer finger in sand, salt, or sugar is an alternative form of this practice that is kinesthetically grounding.

2. Model for the client the process of breathing into the diaphragm for a count of five, holding your breath for a count of five, and releasing your breath slowly for a count of five.

3. Model breathing in for a count of five while drawing a five-point star, holding your breath for a count of five while drawing a second five-point star, and breathing out for a count of five while drawing a third five-point star.

4. Invite the client to draw three stars while moving through the breathing cycle. A dry-erase board could also be used for quick drawing and erasure. The *Five-Count Breathing* template can be copied to serve as a practice worksheet.

FIVE-COUNT BREATHING TEMPLATE

5.3 WEIGHED DOWN

DESCRIPTION:

Clients with big behaviors often store stress, energy, aggression, or excitement in their bodies prior to an escalation. These clients can benefit from learning how to intentionally release their pent-up energy. This exercise pairs progressive muscle relaxation with the heaviness of large stones to concretize the process of relaxing their physical bodies.

TREATMENT GOALS:

- Soothe the physiology
- Practice downregulation through progressive muscle relaxation

MATERIALS NEEDED:

- A soft flooring surface
- Large gemstones* or river rocks

DIRECTIONS:

1. Invite the client to lay down on their back on a soft surface. Consider offering relaxing music or a change in lighting to help induce the relaxation response.

2. Lead the client in a progressive muscle relaxation exercise—having them alternately tense and relax different groups of muscles—while also inducing heaviness in the client's limbs after each release of tension.

3. Each time the client has cleared the tension from a body part—for example, after they have squeezed up their arm muscles and then released the tension—offer to place a smooth stone or heavy gemstone on that part to mark that is has been cleared.

4. If you are trained in EMDR, spend time further installing the sense of heaviness and relaxation in the client's body before removing the stones.

---

*With young children, using large transparent gemstones in luminescent colors can increase the magical quality of relaxation.

5.4 MODULATE WITH MUSIC

DESCRIPTION:

Children with big behaviors need help learning how to check in with their bodies. This ability to focus on what the inside of your body is experiencing—known as interoception—is a skill that can be mindfully shaped. Musical instruments offer one way for clients to take their internal dysregulation and externalize it. This intervention pairs mindful interoception with the playing of musical instruments.

TREATMENT GOALS:

- Help the client practice interoception
- Externalize body responses through music
- Modulate regulation using musical instruments

MATERIALS NEEDED:

- Musical instruments (e.g., guitar, ukulele, maraca, tambourine, finger clappers)
- Oximeter (or a digital device with a heart rate app)

DIRECTIONS:

1. Begin by having the client check their heart rate with the oximeter or digital app.

2. Ask them to turn their focus inside and to notice if they can feel their heart beating.

3. Invite the client to play the musical instrument in the rhythm they experience.

4. Ask the client to slow down the external rhythm and see if it can impact the internal rhythm. Check their heart rate again.

5. Engage in some exciting behavior—such as jumping jacks, burpees, or a dance party—and invite the client to use the musical instrument to express the pace at which their heart is beating now.

6. Play with these patterns, moving from interoception to external musical expression and vice versa.

5.5 YOGA TUNES

DESCRIPTION:

Dysregulated children benefit from practices that calm the body and center the mind. Yoga can do both, but hyperkinetic children can lose focus quickly during traditional yoga practice. This exercise invites the client to choose a yoga pose while pairing the holding of the pose with the resolution of a sound, offering two areas of mindful focus at the same time.

TREATMENT GOALS:

- Increase mindfulness practice
- Pair the stillness of the pose with a sound (pairing auditory and kinesthetic focal points)

MATERIALS NEEDED:

- Illustrations/instructions for yoga poses, like the *Yoga Pretzels* card deck (Gruber & Kalish, 2005)
- Buddhist chimes or a xylophone

DIRECTIONS:

1. Introduce the client to yoga practice, encouraging them to choose a pose that seems fun to them.

2. Practice the pose in silence first.

3. Explain that you will clink the chimes together (or play the xylophone) as you both begin to make the pose, and you will hold the pose until you hear the sound fully resolve into silence.*

4. Invite the client to take a turn making the sound while you both make the pose.

5. Explore together the experiential differences between doing the yoga poses in silence and doing the yoga poses paired with a resolving sound.

---

*If the child is having difficulty sustaining the length of time it takes for the sound to resolve, provide an instrument that has a shorter resolve time, such as a drum or a tambourine.

5.6 | SOMATIC SCAVENGER HUNT

DESCRIPTION:

Clients with big behaviors often have a hyperaroused stress-response system that can benefit from somatic grounding. Helping children focus on sensory input from the environment is one way to help them ground in the here and now, creating mindful moments to counter hyperarousal. This exercise can be especially helpful if a client is beginning to dissociate during trauma processing.

TREATMENT GOALS:

- Assist clients in identifying somatic states
- Engage in mindfulness practice related to the five senses

MATERIALS NEEDED:

- Several copies of the *Somatic Scavenger Hunt* handout

DIRECTIONS:

1. Introduce the concept of mindfulness by describing how it has to do with being fully immersed in the present moment.

2. Ask the client to scan the environment for five things they can see, four things they can touch, three things they can hear, two things they can smell, and one thing they can taste. Have them record these things on the *Somatic Scavenger Hunt* handout, writing down their sensory experiences beneath the part of the body that is the portal for that sensory experience (i.e., the things they see are written beneath the eye, and so forth).

3. Offer additional copies of the handout for the client to use at home and at school to practice being mindful in other environments.

SOMATIC SCAVENGER HUNT HANDOUT

Scan your environment for five things you can see, four things you can touch, three things you can hear, two things you can smell, and one thing you can taste. Write your sensory experiences beneath the part of the body that is the portal for that sensory experience.

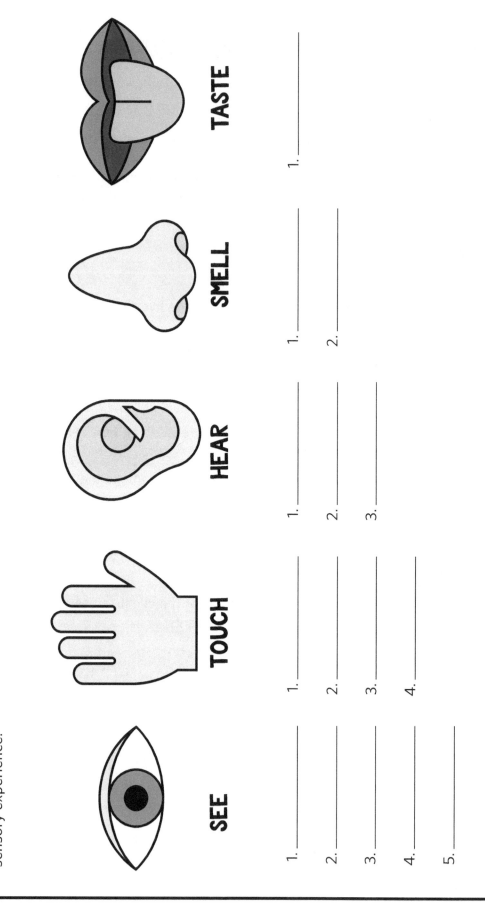

SEE

1. _____
2. _____
3. _____
4. _____
5. _____

TOUCH

1. _____
2. _____
3. _____
4. _____

HEAR

1. _____
2. _____
3. _____

SMELL

1. _____
2. _____

TASTE

1. _____

COOKED AND UNCOOKED SPAGHETTI

DESCRIPTION:

Clients who have underlying anxiety will sometimes engage in big behaviors when their stress-response system is overactivated. These clients tend to hold their bodies more rigidly and need practice in "loosening up." This intervention offers a playful way to do just that.

TREATMENT GOALS:

- Assist clients in identifying somatic states
- Help clients move back and forth between states of full-body tension and full-body relaxation

MATERIALS NEEDED:

- Uncooked spaghetti
- Modeling clay
- Spaghetti extruder tool for the clay
- Chef's hat (or the *Chef's Hat* template and coloring utensils)
- *Cooked or Uncooked?* handout

DIRECTIONS:

1. Introduce the dry spaghetti to the client. Invite the client to feel the spaghetti and perhaps even paint the hard, uncooked strands and create art with it.

2. While the client is working with the spaghetti, it is likely to break. Talk about how carefully the uncooked noodles have to be handled. Explain how their lack of flexibility puts them at risk for being broken more often.

3. Offer the child a chef's hat to wear (or they can color and personalize the *Chef's Hat* template), and explain that you will pretend you are master chefs who can cook the spaghetti to just the right texture—just wiggly enough without becoming mushy.

4. Play together with the modeling clay and the extruder tool to make different thicknesses of spaghetti noodles, exploring their texture, flexibility, and so forth.

5. Compare the stress stored in our bodies to the rigidity of the uncooked noodles, and the discharge of the tension as the cooked noodles.

6. Using the *Cooked or Uncooked?* handout, explore with the client what sorts of stressors lead to tension in their body. Write these on the lines above the uncooked pasta.

7. Then help the client list three ways they can discharge tension from their body, and write these in the blank lines above the cooked spaghetti.

VARIATION:

This activity can be especially fun and playful when done in a group setting. Have each child take turns being the chef (with their personally embossed chef's hat, of course). The other children stand in the middle of a space defined as "the pot of water," and the chef pretends to turn up the heat in the water. The children begin in a stiff posture, then begin to wiggle their bodies all around, and end by collapsing to the floor in a boneless heap.

CHEF'S HAT TEMPLATE

COOKED OR UNCOOKED? HANDOUT

Think about the stressors that lead to tension in your body. Write these above the uncooked pasta. Next, think of three different ways you can discharge tension from your body and write these above the cooked spaghetti.

WHAT HELPS YOU FEEL COOKED OR UNCOOKED?

_____

_____

_____

_____

_____

_____

_____

_____

UNCOOKED	COOKED
Rigid	Flexible

5.8 ROCK-A-BYE BABY

DESCRIPTION:

Breath work is an evidence-based way to bring our bodies back into regulation. Young children may have difficulty engaging in belly breathing, which involves deep inhalations of breath that expand their abdomens. In addition, many children begin to breathe shallowly or too quickly when they become escalated. This intervention offers a nurturing concrete object (a baby doll) as a focal point for the breath work and encourages repetitive practice.

TREATMENT GOALS:

- Assist clients in using breath work to regulate
- Offer an external focal point to practice deep, diaphragmatic breathing

MATERIALS NEEDED:

- Baby doll (or another nurturing object, such as a stuffed animal or a lovie from home)

DIRECTIONS:

1. Introduce the baby doll to the client. Or, if the client has brought a lovie from home, learn the lovie's name and say hello.

2. Explain that the baby doll has trouble falling asleep on its own and that you are going to practice rocking it to sleep with your breathing.

3. Invite the client to lay down on the floor and to place the baby on their stomach.

4. Have them take a deep breath in. The air should expand their belly upward, gently moving the baby higher.

5. Have them slowly release their breath. As they let the air out, their belly should slowly deflate and the baby doll will descend.

6. Have them practice for several minutes in session and during your next several sessions. If you (or the caregiver) can sing a lullaby during this practice, the song itself can begin to be associated with the relaxation response. Eventually the client may begin to experience regulation or begin deep breathing just from hearing the song.

5.9 | COOL AS A CUCUMBER

DESCRIPTION:

When a client's stress-response system has become wired for hypervigilance, it can be difficult for them to truly relax. For example, when given an invitation to close their eyes and turn their focus inward, their eyelids may continue to flutter open. This intervention provides support to reduce hyperarousal while the client experiences some playful pampering.

TREATMENT GOALS:

- Downregulate the client's neurophysiology by pairing somatic stillness with pleasurable sensory experiences

- Help the client (especially the client with a history of neglect or maltreatment) receive nurturing care

MATERIALS NEEDED:

- Paper and drawing utensils

- Cucumber slices*

- Cucumber eye pads

- Cucumber-scented lotion

DIRECTIONS:

1. Introduce the phrase "cool as a cucumber" as one way to talk about the ability to remain calm and regulated even as stressful events may be happening. Ask the client to draw a picture of someone staying "cool as a cucumber" while a stressful situation is occurring. If needed, you can offer examples of stressful situations, such as listening to parents argue, being asked to take sides in a disagreement between friends, facing a math test that seems especially hard, or realizing that the power has gone out.

2. Explain that the cucumber has a thick skin that protects its cool middle. Offer the client actual slices of fresh cucumber and participate in tasting it with them. Invite the client to notice the smell, the crunch, the difference in texture between the fleshy seeds and the outer skin. If any of these are pleasurable for the client, further install the sensory experience with EMDR (if you are trained).

3. Playfully pretend that you and the client are in a spa environment and explain that the client will get to be pampered with cucumber treatments. Begin by offering cucumber eye pads, as these may provide a counterconditioning response as the client welcomes the extra heaviness on their eyelids.

---

*Check with the caregiver in advance for allergies (to cucumbers or other ingredients in the spa items).

4. Then offer cucumber-scented lotion. Explain that the lotion will help their skin smell good and feel soft, but they can imagine that the lotion is actually thickening their skin so that other people's angry words can't get through as easily. Ask the child where they would like the lotion placed. The hands are often a preferred area; you can provide a hand massage while inviting deeper relaxation for the client.*

VARIATION:

Progressive muscle relaxation exercises can be added to this ritual, as well as breath work. When a safe and grounded caregiver can be taught this playful intervention, more full-body experiences of supported relaxation can happen at home.

---

*It is important to conduct a thorough biopsychosocial interview during the assessment phase of treatment prior to offering lotion and nurturing touch. Some children will have had boundary violations such as physical or sexual abuse, or intrusive medical procedures. In all these circumstances, a focus on bodily autonomy takes priority over the intervention. In a case where you have this concern, this intervention should only be offered after other work around boundaries and trust building in relation to receiving touch has been completed. A safe caregiver can also be invited into the activity to provide the nurturing touch if appropriate. If the use of lotion would be contraindicated in your clinical judgment, you can offer a hand or foot massage instead. Or if the association between touch and relaxation would be contraindicated, you can simply leave this part of the intervention out.

5.10 HUM BUGS*

DESCRIPTION:

This is a creative activity that helps clients connect a concrete object to the mindfulness and self-regulation skills they've learned. It further serves as a visual and kinesthetic tool for practicing soothing vocalizations, like humming or *ohm*-ing.

TREATMENT GOALS:

- Help the client achieve a state of focused relaxation and calming by activating the vagus nerve via humming
- Increase self-empowerment and feelings of control over one's mind and body
- Provide an opportunity for co-regulation between the client and a safe adult who can join in this self-regulation activity
- Strengthen the client's understanding of and appreciation for the mind-body connection

MATERIALS NEEDED:

- Small stones
- Fabric paint
- Googly eyes
- Craft glue
- Various other craft supplies to be used for decorations

DIRECTIONS:

1. Explain that humming or *ohm*-ing is one way to calm the body and mind, so today you will be making hum bugs together.

2. Select rocks to use for creating the hum bugs. Rocks may be found outside during a mindfulness walk with the client if you are able to do this at your practice location. Otherwise, you can purchase rocks at a craft or dollar store in advance. The rocks should be small enough to fit in a pants, coat, or backpack pocket. The client should select two rocks (one for each hand).

3. Provide the client with various craft materials of different colors and textures that they can use to create their hum bugs. Encourage them to mindfully select craft items and identify as many of the five senses as possible in their selection.

4. Once the hum bugs are complete and dried, brainstorm with the client situations in which they may need to calm and regulate themselves at home or school.

5. Invite the client to gently squeeze one hum bug in each hand as they focus on humming or *ohm*-ing together with you or a safe caregiver. They may also practice grounding themselves by visually noticing the colors and textures of their hum bugs. After a few rounds of humming or *ohm*-ing, process how this activity made their brain and body feel.

*Created by Eleah Hyatt, MA, LMFT, RPT. Reprinted with permission from *Parents as Partners in Child Therapy: A Clinician's Guide* (Goodyear-Brown, 2021).

5.11 STILL-THE-STRUGGLE SOCKS

DESCRIPTION:

Children who have experienced trauma can have their neurophysiology wired for hypervigilance. Their internal alarm systems get stuck, much like a doorbell pushed in for too long. Even when they want to relax, their bodies remain vigilant. This intervention can be particularly helpful for children who struggle to close their eyes and relax due to the fear of impending danger.

TREATMENT GOALS:

- Provide psychoeducation about our stress-response system
- Normalize hypervigilance as a response to trauma
- Provide an experience of soothing the physiology

MATERIALS NEEDED:

- Dried beans or uncooked rice
- Essential oils*
- Socks with fun prints on them
- Needle and thread

DIRECTIONS:

1. Explain the following:

   "After we have experienced something really stressful or scary, our bodies want to keep us from feeling that scared or stressed again. You may stay on guard, constantly scanning the environment for signs of danger. Your eyes are helping, and even when you want to close them, your eyelids may fight and flutter open. They don't want to close because they worry something might happen while your eyes are closed. This may be your body's way of trying to keep you safe."

2. Ask the client if they want help with keeping their eyes closed. If they are ready to trust you in this way, say:

   "We can help you teach your body that you are safe now, starting with your eyelids. We will make weighted eye socks that you can put on your eyes when you want to keep them closed while relaxing with me."

---

*Check for allergies before using any essential oils.

3. Invite the client to choose a sock, fill it with dried beans or rice, and add several drops of an essential oil that they associate with rest, such as lavender or peppermint. Once they've added everything they'd like to their sock, help them sew up the open end.

4. Invite the client to warm the sock by microwaving it (under supervision and only for a few seconds), and after making sure it's not too hot, place it on their eyelids while you practice deep breathing or engage in mindfulness work.

VARIATION:

You can also invite the client to explore any of the negative self-talk or irrational thoughts that contribute to a lack of felt safety, and then write reassuring truths (such as "You are safe now" or "He can't hurt you now") on small pieces of paper or fabric and embed these in the rice/beans inside the sock.

5.12 RELAXATION REMINDERS*

DESCRIPTION:

The goal of this activity is to create a visual representation of coping strategies to remind clients to relax throughout the day. The pictures provide cues for clients to engage in their coping strategies at times when they are stressed, as well as reminders to practice when they are not stressed. It is important that we teach clients to practice these skills throughout the day, not just when they are in a crisis situation, anxious, or dysregulated, so they know how it feels for their body to be relaxed.

TREATMENT GOALS:

- Create a visual representation of coping strategies to use as cues to relax throughout the day
- Teach clients to practice skills throughout the day to help create body awareness

MATERIALS NEEDED:

- Lined paper and sticky notes for the client's skill list
- Photo pocket pages
- Various scrapbooking paper and magazines for the photo collage
- Glue sticks
- Scissors
- Stickers
- Colored pencils or markers

DIRECTIONS:

1. Ask the client to name various coping strategies they've learned to help them feel relaxed, less anxious, less angry, and so on. Write these down on a piece of paper to create a master list of relaxation strategies. These can include:

   - Reading a book
   - Petting the dog
   - Going for a walk
   - Listening to music
   - Holding something cold
   - Talking to friends or family
   - Coloring
   - Making art or doing crafts
   - Doing yoga or stretching
   - Deep breathing

---

*Reprinted with permission from *Healing with Creativity: When Talking Just Isn't Enough* (Zouaoui, 2018).

126

2. Explain that in this activity, they will be creating a collage of photos representing their adaptive coping strategies. These will function as relaxation reminders.

3. With the client's list close by, introduce all the craft materials you have available to use.

4. Next, show the client an example of a completed photo collage. Then plan out what the client would like to include in the different areas of the photo pockets. For example, if the client wishes to cut out a book to represent the adaptive coping strategy "read a book" from their master list, have them rewrite this phrase on a sticky note and place it on the photo pocket, marking the spot until they have found the magazine picture they want to put there.

5. In the first pocket, place their name (this can be done with stickers, stencils, or drawing).

6. Repeat the process of identifying which strategy goes in which pocket until all pockets are labeled.

7. Introduce a variety of magazines, and invite the client to explore the pictures until they find an image that feels right, then have them cut it out and replace the sticky note with the image.

VARIATION:

If you do not have photo pockets available, the client may collage onto colored index cards and place them on a larger paper or create a flipbook with them.

ADAPTATION FOR TELEHEALTH:

The client can create their collage in Jamboard™ with G-Suite™. They can print it out at home and utilize it in the same way as the other relaxation reminders.

5.13 ZIP... BUT DON'T FLIP!

DESCRIPTION:

Children with big behaviors can flip their lids when excited. Their stress-response systems can't always discern the difference between excitement or anticipation and danger. This game offers a playful way for clients to anticipate a loud sound or action and prepare for it. It also offers a way to pair eye contact with a sense of increasing competency and the payoff of pleasure.

TREATMENT GOALS:

- Practice opening and closing circles of communication
- Expand the client's window of tolerance for distress by offering cycles of upregulation and downregulation while engaged in playful interaction
- Practice self-regulation strategies in response to anticipatory anxiety

MATERIALS NEEDED:

- The Zip Ball by Toysmith®

DIRECTIONS:

1. Explain how this fast-paced back-and-forth ball game works. Each person holds the two handles on their end of the strings. The wider you stretch the grips, the farther you push the ball in the direction of your partner. If you pull the grips apart quickly, it sends the ball zipping over to your partner. In the traditional game, each partner quickly takes turns opening their arms to send the ball back and forth without coming to a stop at either end.

2. Explain that the sender has to ask, "Ready?" and the receiver has to say yes (or give a nod with eye contact) before the sender hurls the ball toward their partner.

3. Invite the client to send you the ball first. If you keep your grips together in front of you, the ball comes hurtling from your partner and makes a loud noise as it slams against the grips. Explain how Amy G. Dala may perceive danger as the ball comes slamming into your grips. Over time, you can desensitize, soothe, and train Amy to know the difference between real danger and perceived danger.

4. Say out loud, "Wow! That was a big noise! Even though I knew it was coming, my body still got scared when it landed with such force! I had to tell myself that I was okay, that I could handle the force of it. Let me take a breath!" Model regulating yourself through breath work.

5. Ask the client if they are ready, and send the ball hurtling back.

6. Practice repetitions of preparing to give and receive the ball, while also practicing regulating in the wake of the loud slam.

VARIATION:

This game can also be used as a way for partners to communicate with each other. One partner (caregiver or therapist) can write an affirmation on a sticky note, stick it to the plastic ball that travels along the cords, and shuttle it over to the child. The child can then read the sticky note, write their own affirmation, and send a response back.

DESCRIPTION:

Children with big behaviors have trouble regulating their physical bodies. Their sense of exteroception (how their body interprets the world around them) is often compromised, and they need support in becoming curious about how their bodies experience the outer world. These clients can benefit from mindful exploration of nature.* This intervention encourages focused attention to the natural environment and invites the client to engage in visual, tactile, olfactory, auditory, and even gustatory experiences while becoming curious about their effects on the body.

TREATMENT GOALS:

- Offer the regulatory benefits of the natural environment to the client
- Enhance the client's practice of mindfulness by bringing increased attention to elements of the natural environment
- Help the client practice grounding themselves with the objects chosen as part of the mindful meal

MATERIALS NEEDED:

- Paper plate (or the *A Mindful Meal* handout) and a writing utensil
- Access to nature, even if it consists of a patch of grass

DIRECTIONS:

1. Take a paper plate and draw lines on it to divide it into six sections. Label each part of the plate with "Something..." (Alternatively, you can use the *A Mindful Meal* handout.)

2. Explain to the client that you are going on a mindfulness walk, and you will be hunting for several things. Together, decide on the "something" categories. Examples include something rough, something smooth, and something small.

3. Along the way, as you pick up each item, have the client notice the visual attention that was needed to find it. Invite exploration of how it looks (smooth rocks can glisten in the sun), feels (moss can feel fuzzy), smells (flowers can smell sweet), sounds (dried leaves can crinkle), and in some cases, tastes (some clients find honeysuckle and want to taste the nectar, or they might just imagine what something tastes like).

4. Reflect on how their bodies feel at different points during the walk.

5. Invite the client's caregivers to have similar mindful meals at home.

---

*Before introducing this activity, make sure that enough trust has been established in the therapist-client relationship that it feels safe to both of you to explore the natural world together (Goodyear-Brown, 2019).

A MINDFUL MEAL HANDOUT

Take this plate on a nature walk and find an item in each category.

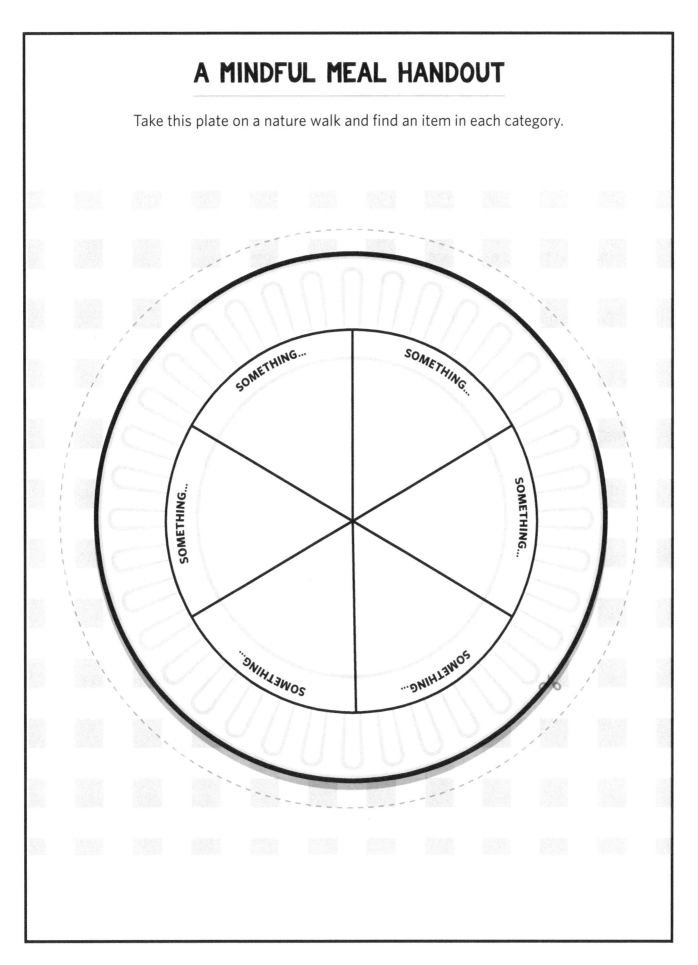

FINESSING THE FEEL

DESCRIPTION:

Once clients with big behaviors start to feel the benefits of mindfulness work and the power of play, they will begin creating interventions all by themselves. While I was on a mindfulness walk in the fall with a teenage client, the client noticed a fruit and vegetable stand along the route. She asked to stop and explored the many piles of gourds and pumpkins. Out of this experience came the following intervention.

TREATMENT GOALS:

- Practice mindfulness with focused tactile attention

MATERIALS NEEDED:

- Three of almost any category of object (gourds, rocks, seashells, jewels, fruits, etc.)—just ensure that there is enough variance between the three chosen items

DIRECTIONS:

1. Offer the three objects in the same category for the client to touch and feel.

2. Explain that when we rely on just one of our senses to explore something, it requires more focused attention and essentially provides us a more mindful experience of the objects.

3. Invite the client to close their eyes and offer them one object at a time, saying, "That's number one, this is number two, and here comes number three." Ask them to identify what each object is. If the client is hesitant to go first, invite them to play the game with you. Close your eyes and let them choose the items to hand to you in order. Then offer them a turn.

4. Begin with objects that are different enough from one another that the client will successfully label the objects. This creates a competency surge that mitigates the client's approach to the next, more similar set of objects. You can up the challenge as you deem appropriate.

5.16 I CAN CALM MY BODY*

DESCRIPTION:

In this activity, the client and therapist will create a book together that includes pictures of the client making faces that express a variety of feelings. Other pages will represent self-soothing strategies the client uses at home when feeling each of these feelings. This activity takes place over several sessions and requires the help of the caregiver at home in between sessions. This intervention can be completed with a child individually, though inviting the caregiver into session can help increase delight between the child and caregiver.

TREATMENT GOALS:

- Increase emotional literacy
- Improve emotional regulation and co-regulation techniques
- Increase attachment between the caregiver and child

MATERIALS NEEDED:

- Eight to ten sheets of paper and/or cardstock
- Camera if using photos of the client**
- Coloring utensils
- Glue or tape
- Stickers, ribbon, or other decoration materials
- Laminate (if desired)
- Hole punch and string, ribbon, or O-rings to bind the book

DIRECTIONS:

1. Explain that the client will be creating a book to illustrate all the different feelings they have and the activities they can use to help themselves feel calm and safe.

2. Invite the client to create a title page for their book.

3. Invite the client to create a list of feelings (offer a list as needed).

4. Invite the client to pose for pictures, expressing each feeling word through facial expressions. This could be done in session or by the client's caregiver at home.

---

*Created by Dayna Sykes, LPC-S, MHSP, RPT.

**Consent from their guardian is needed to use photos. If you cannot use photos, provide pre-cut images from magazines for the child to choose from or invite the child to draw their own illustrations.

5. Invite the caregiver to take photos of the client engaging in self-soothing activities while at home (e.g., cuddling on the couch with the caregiver, playing with a favorite toy, reading a book with the caregiver, resting).

6. Print the photos and invite the client to tell a story for each photo, beginning with an emotional expression. For example, the client looks at the picture that illustrates anger and describes a time they became angry. You may write down the story for the client as they tell it.

7. Invite the client (and the caregiver, if present) to tell a story about using a calming activity when they feel that emotion (e.g., using deep breathing when they feel angry).

8. Repeat for each emotion and calming activity.

9. Assist the client in binding the book together.

10. Ask the client and/or caregiver to read the book aloud in session.

11. Give the client the book to take home with them, and encourage them to read it each day with their caregiver.

5.17 ROLL THE REGULATION DICE*

DESCRIPTION:

This is a method taught and rehearsed in sessions, with the child alone or with their caregiver. Like most interventions for self-regulation, rehearsal and repetition are key components to internalizing new behaviors. The goal is for the child to create a space to be upset, associate emotions with their ability to manage them, begin to distance anger and work toward resolution, and internalize their capacity to do so.

TREATMENT GOALS:

- Teach children self-regulation
- Practice adaptive social interaction skills
- Rehearse resolution-oriented thinking

MATERIALS NEEDED:

- One die

DIRECTIONS:

1. Together, create a sheet titled "I Wonder What My Solution Will Be," in which you help the child (and the caregiver) recall instances that occurred in the recent past that were very upsetting, eventually working their way down to those that were mildly upsetting.

2. Have the child assign a number to each event to reflect how angry or upset they felt at the time, with 1 being "least upset" and 6 being "most upset." It may be best to first write down as many upsetting events as possible and to *then* let the child assign the numbers. They can use the same number for more than one incident.

3. It is important to respect the number that the child chooses—please do not tell them that their number is an exaggeration. The goal is to support the child so they feel safe expressing their emotions, confident that their caregiver is attuned to them, and empowered to seek solutions, problem-solve, and manage their emotions. For example:

"Libby got more cereal than I did." – 2	"You didn't let me take another turn." – 4
"But Dad said *he* would take me." – 3	"I wasn't ready for the math quiz." – 5
"You said I had more time on the iPad." – 6	"Mommy said she would color with me and didn't." – 3
"I didn't want to sit next to Sam." – 1	"Meg took my pen." – 1
"You said I could play longer." – 4	"You said, 'Get out of my room!'" – 5

*Adapted from *Self-Regulation Strategy Using Dice* by Heal with Neal (King, 2020).

4. Once you write down all the events, organize them by grouping them under general themes, so as to have a reference for other triggers that are similar. For example:

1 Not always getting my way: • "I didn't want to sit next to Sam." **Not feeling respected:** • "Meg took my pen."	2 Things that do not feel fair: • "Libby got more cereal than I did."
3 Feeling disappointed: • "Mommy said she would color with me and didn't." • "But Dad said *he* would take me."	4, 5, 6 Feeling angry: • "You said I could play longer." • "You didn't let me take another turn." • "I wasn't ready for the math quiz." • "You said, 'Get out of my room!'" • "You said I had more time on the iPad."

5. Take an example that elicited a 4 or higher. Let the child know that the goal is to use the die to show you the intensity of their feelings and to identify how many breaths it may take to get to a number where they can start to problem-solve (or ask you for help finding a solution).

6. Use the following example as a script for what you will teach and rehearse:

   "Let's see if you can calm your mind and find solutions. When we are really upset, we need to calm down before we can start to problem-solve. The more intense our feelings are, the longer it may take for us to calm down, but when we stick together, we can come up with options to solve the problem. I see you picked a 5 for [*upsetting event*]. Now, take a deep breath and say, 'I wonder what my solution will be?' Take as many breaths as you need before turning the die to 4 and once again say, 'I wonder what my solution will be.' Keep repeating this phrase and turning the die until you get to a 1 or feel like you're ready to begin problem-solving."

7. Encourage the child to rehearse this exercise daily.

VARIATION:

Try referencing other people in the child's life. For example: "What do you think your sister's number would have been yesterday when she started screaming at you about taking her brush?" Doing this can help "warm up" children who are hesitant or unsure about their own experiences—and it can also help build perspective-taking skills.

Impulse Control and Anger Management

For children with big behaviors, impulse control issues often go hand in hand with anger management problems. These clients often experience an overwhelming physiological urge to hit, kick, or throw something when they experience frustration, irritation, disappointment, or anger in their bodies. The comorbidity of these two treatment issues is not surprising. Many of us feel the desire to lash out when we experience big emotions, but our neocortex usually takes over and processes the potential pros and cons of taking an aggressive action. However, for clients who already struggle with executive function—such as those with ADHD, depression, PTSD, fetal alcohol syndrome, or autism spectrum disorder—it can be difficult to step back and do a cost-benefit analysis of acting out, causing them to release this frustrated buildup of energy in the body. Therefore, this chapter includes a variety of self-control games that help clients intentionally freeze and then release—such as freeze dance and red light, green light—to playfully build executive function skills.

When clients struggle to control their anger, it is also important for them to first understand how their bodies are telling them they are angry. Do their fists clench? Do their teeth grind? Does their brow furrow? When the client is able to recognize the early warning signs of energy building up in their body, it is much easier to release the anger appropriately. For example, a six-year-old who is bouncing his knee up and down in agitation—in an attempt to release some energy while still sitting in his desk—may benefit from understanding that this is his body's low-level way of alerting him to the need for movement. If he ignores that need (and so does his teacher), it is likely to morph into an intrusion into a classmate's space, which then frequently escalates to anger. This chapter therefore includes interventions that enhance clients' ability to recognize their anger escalation pattern. In many ways, body-based anger de-escalation work is simply an extension of the self-regulation work that clients learned through the interventions in the previous chapter.

Emotional granularity is another concept that becomes critical in anger management work. In contrast to more vulnerable emotions—like hurt, loneliness, confusion, overwhelm, helplessness, guilt, and shame—anger is an emotion that is easy to identify and powerful to feel. As a result, some of the interventions in this chapter will work on enhancing emotional granularity around anger to uncover any underlying emotions that the anger may be masking.

Finally, it is important to remember that when toddlers knock over their block tower in frustration, they are doing so because they haven't yet learned how to express that feeling verbally. When children learn how to verbally articulate their anger—to simply name the emotion they are experiencing—it brings some cognitive control to the experience of anger. Therefore, once you have helped children identify that anger is present, you can playfully practice using words instead of actions to communicate the feeling. Several interventions in this chapter help with the practice of communicating anger.

TROUBLING TASK TIMER

DESCRIPTION:

Children with big behaviors often act out the most when they are asked to do low-interest activities, like daily chores or personal hygiene tasks. This activity pairs a novel stimulus (a homemade timer) with a fun challenge (a timed trial) while focusing clients to complete the task quickly.

TREATMENT GOALS:

- Create an external focal point for breath work
- Provide external support for timed tasks that require focused attention

MATERIALS NEEDED:

- Two clear plastic ornaments (create-your-own Christmas tree ornaments)
- Super glue or hot glue
- Permanent marker
- Salt or sand
- A piece of paper
- A thin plastic lid from a to-go container
- Scissors
- Cardboard squares
- Dowels or straws
- *Troubling Task Timer* handout

DIRECTIONS:

1. Explain to the client that you will be making a timer together. Invite them to choose two plastic ornaments and remove the center caps.

2. Using the plastic lid of a to-go container (or another thin plastic item), turn one of the ornaments facedown on the thin plastic and use the marker to draw a circle around the top edge. Cut the circle out, and poke a small hole in the middle of it. (The hole can be made bigger at any time, but you can't make it smaller after it has been poked.) Glue this piece to the opening of the ornament.

3. Using a funneled piece of paper, pour salt into the other ornament. Experiment with letting the salt pour through the hole to the second ornament (holding them together) while counting with the client the number of seconds. Timers can be made to count two minutes, five minutes, or more.

4. Adjust the amount of salt and the size of the middle hole until the timer runs for the agreed-upon length of time.

5. Glue the two ornaments together.

6. Set the glued ornaments on a cardboard square slightly bigger than the ornament.

7. Attach straws or dowels (cutting to size) near all four corners of the cardboard. Glue in place and add a final cardboard square on top.

8. Using the *Troubling Task Timer* handout, make a list of tasks that the client might do using the timer—for example, making their bed or completing several sets of multiplication tables in two minutes.

9. Practice this in session by choosing simple tasks the client can complete in the allotted time, such as straightening up your toys or organizing their backpack.

TROUBLING TASK TIMER HANDOUT

Fill in the blanks with tasks you can complete before the timer runs out!

6.2 CONDUCTING CHAOS

DESCRIPTION:

When children carry diagnoses related to inattention or impulse control, they benefit from repetition and fun rehearsal of tasks that require focused attention. In this game, each person in a group (e.g., family, classroom) is given a piece of colored felt and an instrument. Each person gets to take a turn being the conductor and giving cues for the musical instruments to start and stop.

TREATMENT GOALS:

- Increase focused attention to tasks

- Pair attentional tasks with cooperative group work

MATERIALS NEEDED:

- Pieces of colored felt (two pieces of each color; one color for each participant)

- A musical instrument for each participant

DIRECTIONS:

1. Give each participant a colored piece of felt and instruct the group members to place their piece of felt on the floor in front of them and to stand or sit behind it.

2. Let each child choose a musical instrument. If there are not enough musical instruments to go around or if you would rather use self-made sounds, ask each participant to come up with a sound (clicking their tongue, whistling, clapping in rhythm, etc.).

3. Model being the conductor yourself first. The conductor has a colored piece of felt to match each color on the floor. When you hold up a color, the person with that color starts playing their instrument. When you put that color down (or behind your back), they must stop playing immediately. Sometimes you may hold up two colors at once—they both play. If you put one down, that one stops playing but the other continues. You may also hold the colored felt up higher for louder sounds and move it down toward the ground for quieter sounds.

4. Invite different members of the group to become the conductor.

5. Process the intervention with the group members, becoming curious about what it felt like to be the conductor.

    a. How was it when people watched carefully and instantly started or stopped?

    b. Did anyone ever feel ignored during the exercise?

    c. What did it feel like to have to watch the conductor closely for cues?

6.3 | GLOW-IN-THE-DARK FREEZE DANCE

DESCRIPTION:

Clients who have poor impulse control can benefit from playful games that pair immediate acts of self-control with feelings of competence. This game encourages repetitions of self-control after moments of excitation while capitalizing on the novelty of the glow sticks.

TREATMENT GOALS:

- Practice impulse control through play
- Generalize impulse control to other environments

MATERIALS NEEDED:

- Glow sticks (or glow necklaces, bracelets, glasses, wands, etc.)
- Music source and speaker
- Flashlight

DIRECTIONS:

1. Make sure the session takes place in a room that will be pitch black once the lights are turned off (preferably one without windows, or you could use blackout curtains).* With the lights still on, offer the client (or group) glow sticks and notice together the sounds made as the sticks are cracked and the colors that begin to glow.

2. Give the client control of the flashlight as you turn the lights out for the first time.

3. Instruct the client to turn the flashlight off as their signal for you to start the music, and ask them to dance until you stop the music. Their goal is to freeze as soon as they hear the music stop. Whether or not your client has frozen will be quickly evident as you watch their glow sticks.

4. As you "DJ" the freeze dance, alternate between upbeat music that is likely to create an excitation response in the body and calming music that is likely to create a downregulating response. It's helpful to have a playlist created in advance.

5. Afterward, process the skills needed to freeze their bodies in the middle of having fun, such as paying close attention with their minds while their bodies are moving, focusing on the auditory experience, and using self-control (practicing cognitive control over their body's movement).

6. Discuss how these skills may be generalized to other environments. For example, the client can bring this same level of focus when attempting to concentrate on a single detail (e.g., a math problem) in a noisy classroom. Or they can notice when anger is rising in their body and exert self-control instead of impulsively sticking their foot out to trip their peer.

---

*Some children might be fearful of doing this activity in a darkened room. While this fear may represent a separate treatment need, this activity could also be done in a lit room or outside during daylight hours.

6.4 COUNT THE COST

DESCRIPTION:

Children with attentional issues can sometimes focus on a task when there is little outside distraction but become easily distracted with the stimulation of other sounds in the classroom or by family noises while trying to do schoolwork at home. This simple game requires only a set of cards and your best attempts to distract the client, which will help them practice intensifying their focus.

TREATMENT GOALS:

- Provide practice of focusing attention
- Increase the client's ability to tune out distractions

MATERIALS NEEDED:

- A deck of cards (giant or miniature sets can be a fun novelty; alternatively, coins or fake money could be used)

DIRECTIONS:

1. Normalize how difficult it can be to focus when there is a lot going on around us.

2. Explain that you will be practicing extreme focused attention in this game.

3. Give the card set to the client, and tell them their job is to count out loud as they move the cards one by one from their hand to the table. They must also keep their eyes on the cards the whole time.

4. As the client counts the cards, try to distract them with loud noises, maintaining physical proximity, asking questions, or counting in a different numerical order than how the client is currently counting.

5. Celebrate their success if they are able to make it all the way through the stack. For a client with a very short attention span, you might start by using only 10 or 20 cards instead of the whole deck to help the client gain a sense of mastery. In future rounds, you can provide more challenge by upping the number of cards they count.

6. Process the skills needed to stay hyperfocused and identify other tasks and environments in which these skills would be helpful. Discrete behaviors might include keeping their eyes focused entirely on the cards, counting and moving quickly in a continuous fashion, tuning out other noises, or ignoring their peripheral visual input.

VARIATION:

This can be a fun group activity, with the group members all trying to distract the person counting cards. Some boundaries might have to be set with the group members—it is not okay to touch the person counting cards or to use insults of any kind.

RED LIGHT, GREEN LIGHT SCRIBBLE*

DESCRIPTION:

This is an impulse control activity that can be done in a family session or with a group of kids in the classroom. The intervention is meant to increase the use of collaborative skills, increase focus, and promote flexibility within systems. While the scribble game is a tried-and-true play therapy technique, the addition of the storytelling element provides a perfect adaptation to assess current dimensions of the family or group functioning.

TREATMENT GOALS:

- Improve impulse control and the ability to self-regulate
- Improve listening skills, eye contact, and focus
- Promote flexibility and collaboration skills
- Enhance creativity and problem-solving

MATERIALS NEEDED:

- Large piece of paper
- Markers (or other coloring utensils)

DIRECTIONS:

1. Place the paper and markers on the table or floor. Ensure there is enough space for each family member to reach the paper comfortably.

2. The first part of the activity is based on Winnicott's (1971) Interactive Squiggle Game. Have each person pick a marker, and ask one person to draw a scribble on the paper. Then have the next person connect to where the last person left off and add their own scribble. This scribble becomes continuous lines of connections, and the lines can go in whatever direction they choose.

3. Then say, "This is too easy, so we are going to make it harder!" Instruct them to turn the paper over. Ask who knows the game *Red Light, Green Light*. Then explain that in this version of the game, red means stop, green means go, yellow means slow down, and purple means super fast.

4. Assign one person to start out being the leader, and a different person to be the one who starts drawing. Explain that participants will still be playing a game of connecting scribbles, but this time, the person drawing has to follow the leader's direction.

---

*Adapted from *Red Light, Green Light Scribble* (Van Hollander, 2011).

This means the first person to draw cannot start drawing until the first leader says, "green light." Each leader can only give one direction, of their choice:

- **Red:** Stop drawing (or do not start drawing).
- **Yellow:** Draw more slowly.
- **Green:** Start drawing (or continue drawing).
- **Purple:** Draw more quickly.

Then the person to their left becomes the leader. Continue around the circle in this manner. Once several rounds have been played, switch directions.

5. Next, invite them to use the markers and whatever other art supplies they want to create a picture from the scribble. They can color in any images they see and expand on them. This is a fun time for the family or group to work together, quiet their minds, reset, and just color together.

6. After their picture feels complete, ask them to create a story together. Have them go around in a circle, while looking at the picture, and create a "once upon a time" story. Each person says a sentence, but at the end, allow the children to choose their own ending.

You can then ask questions like:

- What was the title?
- What was your favorite part of the story?
- Did they face any obstacles?
- Did they need any resources?

For little ones, you may ask questions like:

- Who were the helpers?
- What created difficulties?

7. Invite everyone to sign the picture using a special "code name" (for confidentiality purposes) and hang it up or allow a member of the family/group to take it home.

ADAPTATION FOR TELEHEALTH:

Using the Zoom whiteboard, take turns using the annotate feature to add scribbles. Once a full scribble has been made, the therapist can act as the scribe, using a text box to type the story onto the same whiteboard. The therapist can save the final creation. Eventually, a whole book of images and stories can be created and shared with the family or group.

6.6 | ANGER BUTTONS

DESCRIPTION:

This technique is useful in helping clients become more aware of the situations or interpersonal interactions that trigger big behaviors, while helping them identify their body's signals that anger is present. Clients will identify how their body communicates to them that they are angry and pair these signals with situations that contribute to anger and aggression.

TREATMENT GOALS:

- Help the client identify their anger triggers
- Help the client become aware of somatic holding of anger
- Help the client connect feelings with behaviors

MATERIALS NEEDED:

- Paper and glue (alternatively, pieces of fabric or felt and a needle and thread)
- Markers
- Buttons in various sizes, shapes, and colors, or the *Anger Buttons* handout
- *Anger Buttons Body* handout

DIRECTIONS:

1. Introduce the technique by talking about things that make us angry. Normalize the feeling of being taken over by our anger:

   "Sometimes it can feel like we are not in control of our own anger responses. A friend says something hurtful and before you know it, you've lashed out with your body. I call that an anger button. Sometimes I feel like I have different anger buttons all over me, and all someone has to do is press that button and I blow up."

2. Ask the client to generate examples from their own life.

3. Offer the *Anger Buttons Body* handout, and explain that we can be angry in varying degrees—while someone who rolls their eyes at us may make us feel irritated, it may not make us as angry as someone who calls us a name. Using the *Anger Buttons* handout or your assortment of real buttons, model choosing buttons of different shapes and sizes to reflect varying degrees of anger that you felt in specific situations.

4. Invite the client to focus on a specific situation that causes anger, and ask them to notice where they feel that anger in their body. How does their body tell them they are angry?

5. Have them choose buttons from your collection, or color and cut out buttons from the *Anger Buttons* handout, and then glue these buttons on the *Anger Buttons Body* handout over the parts of the body that hold this anger. For each button, ask them to identify a situation that is often paired with their body's response, and write down this situation on or next to the button itself. For example, a client might place the anger button that represents "someone making noise during a test" over her mouth, because it irritates her and makes her clench her teeth. She might put another anger button, "someone laughs at me," over her hands, because this usually results in her hitting someone.

VARIATION:

This same exercise can be used to build somatic associations to anxiety. Often, clients may carry anxiety and anger in the same physical locations, and what is actually a manifestation of worry can be confused with anger.

ANGER BUTTONS BODY HANDOUT

Think about something that makes you angry. Focus your thoughts and energy on it. Where do you feel it in your body? Take an anger button and place it in the spot on the body where you feel that anger. On or next to the button, write down the thing or situation that makes you feel angry.

ANGER BUTTONS HANDOUT

Choose which buttons you want to represent how anger shows itself in your body. You can color them in with whatever color you want to represent anger.

 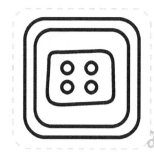 

6.7 WHO'S PRESSING YOUR BUTTONS?

DESCRIPTION:

Clients who are quick to anger and who lack impulse control move from feeling frustrated or disappointed to lashing out physically in an instant. These clients are the ones most likely to be corrected in their classrooms, even when another child may be complicit in the client's escalation. Another student may call them a name, laugh at them, or roll their eyes at them. The client then reacts with aggression or a raised voice, disrupts the classroom, and receives a consequence. This activity gives clients time to look at the connections between other people's actions and their personal power, with the goal of shifting their responses in triggering situations.

TREATMENT GOALS:

- Identify patterns of reactivity (e.g., aggression, yelling)
- Shift the client's paradigm around what personal power looks like
- Practice strategies for distancing themselves from the button pressing of others

MATERIALS NEEDED:

- Completed *Anger Buttons* activity (6.6)
- Toy buttons that play sounds (either prerecorded or that you can record)
- Permanent markers
- Clear plastic (such as cling wrap, cellophane, or plastic baggies cut in half)

DIRECTIONS:

1. Using the *Anger Buttons* activity that was completed previously, begin a discussion with the client of who presses their anger buttons the most—for example, a kid at school who calls the client a loser, which triggers the client to hit the other kid. Explain that you and the client will explore ways to respond instead of reacting.

2. Tell this story:

   "Imagine that there is a kid named Johnny who is having a lot of trouble with his grades. He feels pretty yucky about himself, and one day he sees your math test score, and he sees that your grade is better than his, so he calls you a stupid nerd. If you react to his words by crying, yelling, or telling him he better take it back, he may feel a quick surge of power. He got you to engage with him. He got you to get angry, and that's its own power. Johnny now knows that you have a 'stupid nerd' button. All he has to do is say those words (press that button), and you yell and scream. And guess who gets in trouble? Yep, you, because Johnny made sure his insult was under his breath so he wouldn't attract the teacher's attention."

3. Introduce the toy buttons. Invite the client to push these buttons and see the reaction. You can use prerecorded messages, or you and the client can decide together what to record on them. This can become a playful way to look at the consequences of letting someone else press their buttons. One recording might be the client, in a booming voice, saying, "Go to the principal's office!" Another recording might say, "You will stay inside for recess!"

4. Ask the client to think about who has the power in situations where the client's anger buttons are being pushed—for example, "All he has to do is call you a loser, and you yell mean names back, and then you are the one who gets caught and gets in trouble. Who has the power in that situation?" The answer is the other person.

5. Explain that real power involves backing up from the situation and deciding how to respond.

6. Offer the clear plastic, and cut a sheet that goes over the anger buttons.

7. Over each anger button, write on the plastic wrap a distancing strategy that allows the client to respond instead of reacting.

8. Help the client practice imagining the shield going up that keeps others from pressing their buttons using examples of real-life triggers.

IT'S A CRAP SHOOT

DESCRIPTION:

Children and teens with big behaviors can have difficulty naming their stressors. Their window of tolerance often needs to be stretched to help them reflect on hard things that are happening. This activity pairs discussion of stressors with playful engagement while normalizing how yucky some situations in life can feel.

TREATMENT GOALS:

- Name current stressors that are associated with acting out behaviors
- Identify maladaptive strategies the client uses as a response to anger
- List adaptive replacement strategies

MATERIALS NEEDED:

- Toy slingshot*
- Multiple copies of the *Crap Shoot Target* template
- Markers

DIRECTIONS:

1. Acknowledge that crappy things happen in life. Ask the client to identify some crappy things in their life (defined as situations that feel unjust, unpleasant interactions with people, and other stressors in the client's life). Write each situation on a separate *Crap Shoot Target* sheet.

2. Explain that how we respond to the crappy situation can help it or make it worse.

3. Tape all the targets to the door or wall, displaying the various crappy situations.

4. Have the client pick one of the crappy situations to start with. Ask them to verbally identify an unhelpful (maladaptive) response to that situation.

5. Show them how to pull the band of the slingshot back while holding on tight to the shooter. When they let go of the band, it flies out of the shooter and hits the target.

6. Then ask the client to identify helpful (adaptive) replacement strategies they could use to respond to the situation, and shoot these at the target.** Discuss how the outcome of the situation might change if these strategies are used.

7. Repeat the process of targeting each crappy situation with both unhelpful and helpful responses.

---

*You can even find a slingshot that features the poop emoji to fit the theme of this activity.
**When discussing adaptive strategies, you might use a different emoji slingshot for contrast, such as a smiley face.

VARIATION:

While this adaptation may not be appropriate for everyone, some teenagers respond to a version of this intervention called "When the !@$# Hits the Fan." The slingshot is targeted at a ceiling fan, and the actual consequences of the client's maladaptive anger response patterns ("I got suspended from school," "I got my phone taken away," etc.) are discussed as they engage in this kind of target practice.

CRAP SHOOT TARGET TEMPLATE

UNDER THE ERUPTION

DESCRIPTION:

Children with externalizing behaviors are more likely than their peers to interpret any buildup of stress, anxiety, or tension in their bodies as anger. Anger is a powerful feeling, and children can feel strong while experiencing it. Many of the more vulnerable feelings that are experienced as tension increases are interpreted by the children as weakness. This activity is meant to help children identify the feeling states that may contribute to anger escalation and practice naming these prior to an eruption.

TREATMENT GOALS:

- Increase the client's emotional granularity
- Expand the client's feelings vocabulary
- Name emotions that are more difficult for the client to acknowledge

MATERIALS NEEDED:

- *Anger Volcano* handout
- Stickers

DIRECTIONS:

1. Introduce the client to the idea that anger is a powerful feeling and the easiest to acknowledge when we are in distress. Anger is a good indicator that hurt or other feelings are also present, and when we begin to acknowledge the feelings underneath the anger and ask for help when we are experiencing them, we can avoid escalating and exploding in anger.

2. Introduce the *Anger Volcano* handout and talk about what happens as heat builds up inside a volcano. When it has no way to vent, the pressure eventually gets so intense that it erupts, spewing lava and hot gases everywhere. Discuss how acting out in anger works the same way.

3. Invite the client to name some of the other feelings that lead up to anger. Write these on the lines in the volcano. Provide a list as needed—these feelings might include disappointment, hurt, loneliness, sadness, confusion, overwhelm, frustration, exhaustion, stress, or helplessness. For older children and teens, the feelings may be ranked from the client's experience of intensity of each feeling.

4. Send the completed handout and some stickers home with the client. If they are able to name any of the underlying feelings experienced *before* they explode (even if the explosion still happens), have them put a sticker on the left side of the volcano. If

they have an explosion, but can come back later and, with their thinking brain back on board, name the underlying feelings that led up to the anger, have them put a sticker on the right side of the volcano by each feeling they can name. This is not a positive reinforcement system, but a tracking tool to help both the clinician and the client better understand which emotions are more easily experienced and named, and which may require more exploration or education.

ANGER VOLCANO HANDOUT

In the spaces below, write down the more vulnerable feelings that can build up inside you and eventually lead to an eruption of anger.

6.10 ALIBABA AND HIS BUCKING CAMEL

DESCRIPTION:

Clients with big behaviors live with a dysregulated stress-response system and have little understanding of their own window of tolerance for distress. Many clients who act out in angry or controlling behaviors do so as an outgrowth of underlying anxiety. This intervention helps clients practice breathing through anticipatory anxiety while naming stressors and normalizing that the more stress builds up, the more likely we are to leave our optimal arousal zone.

TREATMENT GOALS:

- Identify current stressors in the client's life
- Practice self-regulation when coping with anticipatory anxiety
- Assist the client in exploring their body's response to sudden sounds and movement

MATERIALS NEEDED:

- Alibaba and His Bucking Camel game
- Paper or sticky notes
- Markers

DIRECTIONS:

1. Help the client become familiar with the game. Demonstrate how the camel is positioned on his knees, then place the saddle and Alibaba on top of the camel.

2. Explain to the client the process of the game. There are five pegs to place items on the camel. The order is given by drawing cards that correspond to the props. When the weight of the objects, influenced by how they were placed, is too much for the camel, it will suddenly spring up. This creates a loud, startling series of noises as the objects fall. Invite the client to experiment with the motion of the camel and its spring.

3. Commence with the game. As you play, have the child think about things that they may have to carry (stressors, worries), just like the camel. Write down the stressors they mention on a piece of paper. Alternatively, you can record them on sticky notes and attach them on the items that will be placed again on the camel.

4. When the camel bucks off its items, help the client to take stock of their bodily reaction to the unexpected alarm of the moment.

5. Help the client identify which parasympathetic responses help them regulate most quickly after their startled reaction. The therapist can even model ways to calm down, like squeezing one's hands or inhaling deeply and exhaling slowly. The child and therapist may end up squeezing each other's hands, closing their eyes in anticipation of the explosive bucking sound, shaking out their bodies after the camel has bucked off all the weight, or laughing loudly as a way to discharge the pent-up tension. All of these responses can be translated into ways the child's body is attempting to regulate itself during and after a stressful event.

6.11 HOW TO DEFUSE A BOMB*

DESCRIPTION:

Clients with big behaviors can experience shame after they have had an anger escalation. This intervention playfully acknowledges the explosive nature of anger reactions while helping the client identify ways to begin changing the pattern.

TREATMENT GOALS:

- Help the client identify when they are about to "blow up"
- Identify ways the client can control their reactions (defuse the bomb)

MATERIALS NEEDED:

- *Bomb Squad* handout

DIRECTIONS:

1. Introduce the idea of a bomb squad to the client.

   "Have you ever heard of a bomb squad? A bomb squad is a team of specially trained individuals who all work together to stop a bomb from exploding and hurting other people. These helpers wear special suits, work together, and use unique tools to stop the bomb from going off and hurting other people."

2. Then help the child identify how their reactions can be similar to a bomb that explodes.

   "I remember when your brother took the toy you were playing with, and you got so angry you hit him. Let's replay this scenario like we are on the bomb squad and see where we could have used our unique tools to defuse the bomb."

3. Explore what the child's thoughts were right before the "explosion."

   "What were you thinking when you were playing with your brother?"

   "This is fun! I love playing blocks with my brother!"

4. Identify what happened next to cause the bomb to "explode."

   "Right before you hit your brother, what happened?"

   "My brother took the block I needed to build my castle."

5. Explore the thoughts related to this incident.

   "When your brother took your block, what were you thinking then?"

   "I will never be able to build a big castle."

---

*Created by Lindsey Townsend, LCSW, and Tasha Jackson, LCSW.

6. Explore the associated feelings and body sensations.

   "How was your body feeling?"

   "Angry. My stomach hurt, and my body was tense."

7. Review what the child said they were thinking and feeling and ask them to describe the "explosion."

   "You were thinking you wouldn't be able to build your castle because your brother took the block. You were feeling angry, and your body was feeling tense. What happened next?"

   "I hit my little brother in the arm."

8. Work with the client to identify the unique tools they can use to defuse future explosions. You can use the *Bomb Squad* handout as a template or a starting point to create the client's personal plan for defusing anger bombs.

   "Okay, let's put on our special protective suits, gather our helpers, and find our unique tools so we can create a plan to stop the next bomb from going off."

9. After you've identified all of the client's helpers and unique tools, invite the caregiver to join the child's team of helpers.

BOMB SQUAD HANDOUT

Your Mission: To safely defuse anger bombs before they go off!

Step 1: Suit Up

Evaluate the situation. Ask yourself:

- What kind of thoughts am I having?

  _____

  _____

  _____

  _____

- How is my body feeling?

  _____

  _____

  _____

  _____

Step 2: Gather Your Squad

Find your helpers so they can support you.

- My helpers:

  _____

  _____

  _____

  _____

Step 3: Defuse the Bomb

Use these tools to defuse the bomb. Keep trying different tools until one works!

- The Four Qs:

    1. *Quiet:* Go to a safe and quiet place.
    2. *Quit:* Quit thinking of negative things.
    3. *Quest:* Go for a walk (a.k.a. a quest)!
    4. *Quad:* Find four things you can see, hear, smell, and touch.

- My unique tools:

_____

_____

_____

_____

ARE YOU READY FOR THE BOOM?

DESCRIPTION:

This intervention helps clients work with their anticipatory anxiety, pairing the anxiety response with a regulation strategy while also naming stressors or anxieties that contribute to explosive behaviors.

TREATMENT GOALS:

- Identify stressors that contribute to explosive behavior

- Make connections between anxiety and anger outbursts

- Practice self-regulation strategies, like deep breathing, to manage anticipatory anxiety

- Help the client understand their own stress-response system

MATERIALS NEEDED:

- Boom Boom Balloon game
- Multiple balloons

- A permanent marker
- One die

DIRECTIONS:

1. Explain that anger can build up when we experience a bunch of other challenging emotions, like frustration, disappointment, confusion, guilt, or shame. When we don't communicate these other feelings safely, the pressure builds up. It can start to feel like if one more thing happens, you will just pop!

2. Follow the directions for assembling the game, and blow up a starting balloon. You can draw an anxious or angry face on the balloon with a permanent marker to help illustrate the game concept.

3. The balloon fills the middle space, and long sticks are placed in nine holes around the frame. These get pushed farther and farther into the middle, pressing against the balloon, until finally it pops.

4. Explain that you roll the die and push the sticks in one click for each number on the die. If you roll a four, you can push one stick in four times or four different sticks in one time each. This becomes an issue of strategy as you try to avoid popping the balloon.

5. For each roll, have the client verbalize one stressor, anxious thought, or hard thing they are experiencing in life currently.

6. As the balloon gets more squeezed on every side, the player's anticipatory anxiety rises. Invite the client to check in with their body, to notice where they are feeling the anxiety, and to breathe through it together. You might even say counterconditioning mantras together, like "My body is ready for it."

7. When the balloon pops, there may be screams, squeaks, and laughter. Check in with how the client's body is responding to this sudden shock.

8. Explore ways to use the skills applied in this game to other life situations.

seven

Emotional Literacy

When children experience dysregulation in the midbrain (the limbic system), it can result in extreme emotions, such as hair-trigger anger, excessive irritability, debilitating anxiety, intense sadness, dissociation, or numbing. Midbrain dysregulation can also take the form of social difficulties, such as excessive bossiness, bullying behavior, extreme shyness, or withdrawal around peers. Expanding the client's feelings vocabulary and emotional granularity provides their own form of midbrain regulation. As we identify feeling words and articulate them verbally, we are actively engaging the neocortex, which brings the power of executive function on board to help mediate the powerful emotion. When a client is able to identify and verbalize a feeling they have been bottling up, it reduces the potential toxicity of that feeling.

Particularly when a client manifests anger in hurtful ways, expanding their emotional vocabulary allows them to name more complex feelings that may stack up prior to an explosion. For clients who have experienced significant trauma, it may be necessary to expand their emotional vocabulary to build narrative coherence. They may also need permission for several big feelings to all be present at the same time (e.g., "I am deeply relieved that my abuser is gone, but I also deeply miss some parts of that person") or that may show up in a progression (e.g., in a grief reaction, where a child may move through several feelings in succession). Clients can also benefit from pairing certain situations with resulting emotions. This can help clients prepare in advance for how they might respond in the moment, while encouraging them to slow down and think through how they want to respond (e.g., get distance, take a breath, use their voice, ask for help).

Helping a child begin the process of labeling their emotions and noticing their physiological indicators can be a powerful coping tool as they grow and mature throughout the lifespan. While equipping children with emotional literacy skills is important, the most effective regulator for big emotions (especially for children who are very young) is a safe and secure co-regulator. Empowering children to signal for support by asking for what they need during moments of distress is an essential life skill that can serve them for years to come. Therefore, this chapter offers a plethora of playful activities that make learning about emotions fun!

7.1 COLOR YOUR HEART

DESCRIPTION:

Clients who exhibit big behaviors often do so because they do not yet have the words to express the feelings coursing through their bodies. Labeling feelings is part of the process of integrating the lower brain regions with the neocortex. This activity can help the client reflect on how often they have felt each of the primary emotions recently, while pairing each emotion with situations that have elicited that emotion. This assessment tool can give the clinician a good understanding of the child's internal emotional world as it stands currently, guide a deeper exploration of trauma processing when traumatic events are tied to these emotions, guide the development of coping skills for difficult feelings, and help uncover which emotions may need to be introduced into the client's feelings vocabulary.

TREATMENT GOALS:

* Explore several primary emotions
* Nonverbally quantify the client's recent experience of these emotions
* Pair these emotions with specific situations

MATERIALS NEEDED:

* *Color Your Heart* script
* Coloring utensils
* White paper or the *Color Your Heart* template

DIRECTIONS:

1. Invite the child to choose five colors while you draw a large heart on a piece of paper and add a legend of five boxes (or use the *Color Your Heart* template).

2. Ask the client to choose a color to represent each of these four primary feelings: happy, sad, mad, and scared.

3. Then ask the client, "What's another emotion that children feel sometimes?" Alternatively, you can ask them to name another emotion that they feel sometimes or name the reason the client is coming to treatment—let's say divorce adjustment—and ask the child to describe how they feel about their parents divorcing.

4. Color in the boxes on the legend to correspond with each of these five feeling words. Then ask the client to color in the heart with each color to describe how much they feel that emotion in their own heart. If the client is open to further work, ask for situations that are tied to each of these emotions and write them over the colors in the heart.

5. This intervention can be used several times during the course of treatment to assess shifts or expansion in emotional literacy.

ADAPTATION FOR TELEHEALTH:

Using an online whiteboard and digital coloring tools, a Color Your Heart can be easily created and saved during virtual sessions.

COLOR YOUR HEART SCRIPT

The following script can be used if needed (spoken words are in bold):

We are going to do an art activity. I'm going to draw a big heart on this sheet of paper while you are choosing five colors from these [*markers/paints/crayons*]. You draw a heart in black ink while the child chooses five colors. Draw five squares in the bottom-left corner to create a legend.

Then say, **Now, which color do you want to be your happy color?** When the child chooses, color in the first box of the legend and either draw a happy face or write out the word *happy*, depending on their developmental age. Then say, **Now, which color do you want to be your sad color?** Repeat this process for mad and scared—these basic four feelings should fill the first four boxes.

The way you structure the exploration of the fifth color/feeling pairing will require your clinical judgment, and it will depend in part on the treatment issue and the child's level of guardedness. If you have a highly defended child, you might just say, **What's another emotion that kids feel sometimes?** This allows for the focus to be generalized. If you have good rapport already, you can ask, **What's another emotion you feel sometimes?** A third option is to begin to bring the treatment issue in the room with this fifth feeling, letting the child know what you know and enhancing their understanding that you can hold it with them. You can say, **I know that your brother died by suicide last week. What's a feeling kids feel when that happens?** It may be helpful to have a feelings chart* of some kind nearby in case children need it for reference.

Once all the colors have been assigned a feeling, say, **Now we are going to color in this heart with as much of each feeling as you have in your own heart. If you were happy all the time, you might color in the whole heart with happy, but I don't know anyone who is happy all the time, do you?** This question is meant to mitigate the child's potential defensive reaction to only color in positive or socially appropriate emotions. If the child responds by insisting that they are "all happy," go with the resistance for now. When the child is done putting as much of each color in the heart as they want, reflect on the colors with them by asking, **Which color takes up the most room in the heart? What are some of the things that make you feel that way?**

---

*You can use the *Feelings Chart* handout on page 186 of this book.

COLOR YOUR HEART TEMPLATE

FEELINGS RHYME BOOK*

DESCRIPTION:

The younger the child with big behaviors, the more important it can be to help them develop emotional literacy. Learning new feeling words and pairing those feelings with specific situations can help leach the intensity out of bodily expressions of big feelings.

TREATMENT GOALS:

- Give the client a basic introduction to emotions so age-appropriate emotional verbalization and expression can occur throughout treatment

- Expand the client's ability to articulate their feelings and connect them to real-life situations

- Help the client identify emotions and build an emotional vocabulary while becoming more aware of physiological indicators that signal an emotion is present

MATERIALS NEEDED:

- Colored and white paper
- *Rhyme Word Page* template

- Stapler
- Scissors

- Glue
- Coloring supplies

DIRECTIONS:

1. Start with a developmentally appropriate iteration of the following script:

   "All people have feelings. Feelings start on the inside of us, and as we learn to understand what our bodies are telling us, we can name these feelings. Naming our feelings helps us stay connected to others and ask for what we need."

2. Share with the child that you will be working together to create a book about emotions and how they show up in the client's body. Discuss the importance of learning how to "listen to your body" as emotions show up on the inside. You may help the client practice these "listening" skills through some mindfulness-based activities.

3. Allow the child to choose the paper color for their book cover and staple together a basic book with six white pages in the middle.

4. Cut out the rhyme prompts from the *Rhyme Word Page* template, and paste each one on a page of the book, in order. Invite the child to print their name on each blank line. The client can then draw a self-portrait to correspond with the rhyme prompt on each page until the book is completed.

5. Read the book together and reflect on real-life situations that activate each feeling state.

6. If possible, invite the client to read their book to their caregiver as an opportunity for them to delight in and communicate with each other. You can also have them invent body movements to go with the rhymes, which they can practice together while facing each other.

---

*Created by Eleah Hyatt, MA, LMFT, RPT.

RHYME WORD PAGE TEMPLATE

This is _____ happy.

This is _____ sad.

Now you see _____ sleepy.

Now you see _____ mad.

Sometimes _____ has big feelings,
and those are hard to hold...

But when _____ learns to ask for help,
_____ grows and feels so bold!

7.3 MOOD MANICURE

DESCRIPTION:

Clients who escalate into aggressive behavior are often lacking a nuanced understanding of their own emotions. They may also have co-regulators who could benefit from expansion of emotional literacy within the family system. This intervention pairs feelings with nail polish colors and invites shared nurturing experiences as big feelings are named and paired with situations that engender each feeling.

TREATMENT GOALS:

- Identify a range of feelings
- Identify connections between specific situations and the client's feelings
- Practice verbalizing statements that pair situations with feelings
- Explore the client's self-perception of the intensity of certain feelings
- Enhance storykeeping between caregiver and client (when used with dyads)

MATERIALS NEEDED:

- Bottles of nail polish in a variety of colors
- Paper towels or a vinyl cloth to protect the furniture and/or flooring
- *Mood Manicure* handout and recording form

DIRECTIONS:

1. Invite the client to choose six bottles of nail polish from your collection and to color each bottle pictured in the *Mood Manicure* handout with one of the colors chosen.

2. Ask the client to pair each color with a feeling, and write the feeling word on the corresponding drawn bottle.

3. Then paint each other's nails—each nail can be painted with any color (of the six) that they choose, but they must give an example of a situation that has engendered that feeling. Clients may want all of their nails painted one color—for example, red. If the client paired red with the feeling of anger, they would describe ten different situations that engender anger. This allows you to see the intensity of the feelings the client has while exploring the emotional lens through which the client views their experiences.

4. As the activity progresses, use the *Mood Manicure* recording form to take notes on the feelings and experiences that the client shares, writing each situation next to the painted fingernail that represents it.

5. Invite client to color in the nails on the handout to match the nails on their hands.*

---

*Nurturing touch is an inherent aspect of this intervention, as careful attention is given to the client's hands. This could be paired with a hand massage, especially when the therapist is facilitating Mood Manicures between a caregiver and a child, in order to further enhance the quality of nurture and delight within the dyad.

MOOD MANICURE HANDOUT

Choose six bottles of real nail polish, then color in the outlines below to match your nail polish colors. Choose a feeling to go with each color of nail polish and write it on the label.

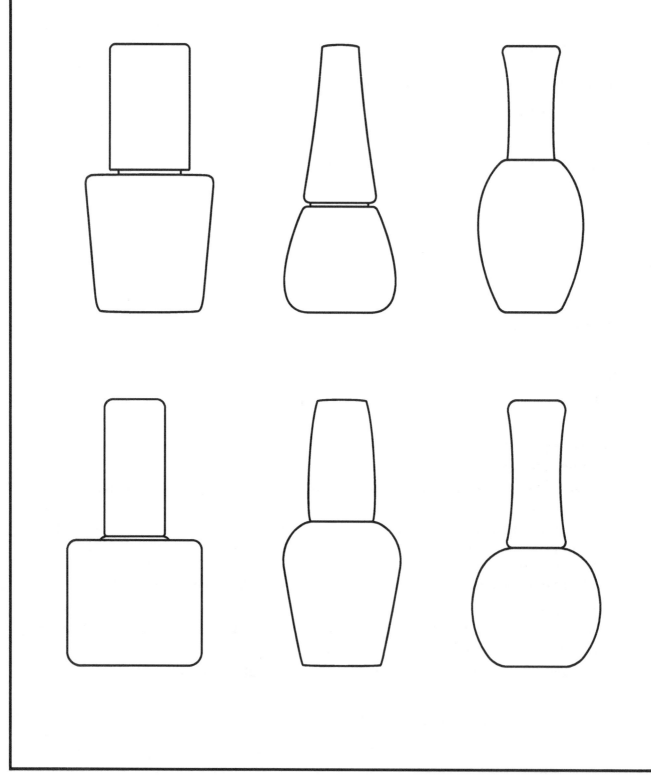

MOOD MANICURE RECORDING FORM

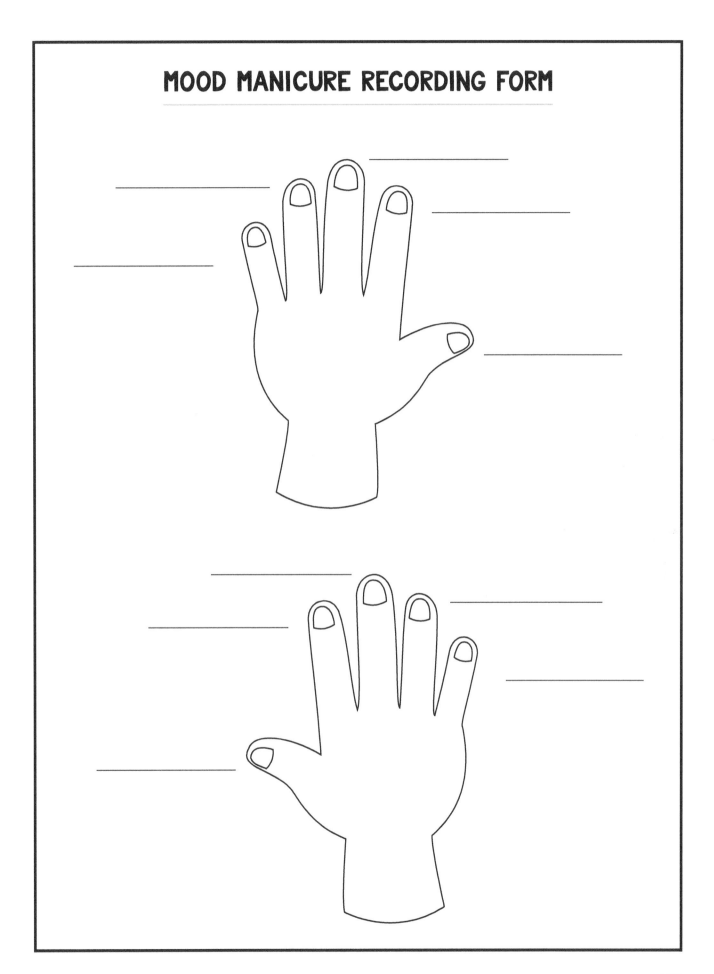

7.4 SANDS OF TIME

DESCRIPTION:

Grief reactions in children and teens often involve behavioral escalations. This intervention can help clients sort through their feelings and create a timeline of emotions, beginning with their first understanding about the loss that was to come and ending with the current moment. This intervention can be used to help clients process the death of a family member, the loss of a house or property due to a natural disaster (such as a tornado or a flood), or a divorce. When this activity is used to process the death of a loved one, the completed sand-art creation can function as a memorial marker for that person.

TREATMENT GOALS:

- Assist the client in reflecting on their grief journey

- Name the emotions in sequence as the client has journeyed through grief

- Normalize the variety and intensity of feelings felt during grief

MATERIALS NEEDED:

- Sand-art bottles in a variety of sizes and shapes (stars, suns, etc.)

- Multiple colors of sand

- A funnel

DIRECTIONS:

1. Explain that grief is a process and that many feelings are experienced from the moment someone learns that a loss is coming, through the loss itself, and into the future.

2. Structure the activity by helping the client sequence the events. For example, a timeline might include the following: (1) Mom and Dad sat me down and told me Mom had breast cancer. (2) Mom had to have a surgery. (3) Mom was too tired to play with me. (4) Mom lost her hair. The list might go on.

3. Invite the client to choose a bottle and to then pair sand colors with feeling words. Beginning with the first event (learning Mom had breast cancer), instruct the client to add sand into the jar for the feeling they felt first. Invite the client to add as much sand as needed to show how much they felt that feeling. Sometimes a client will have so much of one feeling (anger, loneliness, etc.) that they fill up a whole bottle with it. In that case, just reflect on how big that feeling was for them and offer a second bottle.

4. This activity can be especially powerful when done dyadically. The caregiver and child can make bottles together. Sometimes they are the same and sometimes different, validating the variety of ways that children grieve. When the bottle is all finished, it serves as a visual narrative of their emotional journey through grief.

SUPER-FEELING FRUITS AND VEGETABLES

DESCRIPTION:

This intervention offers a playful way for clients to project an emotion that they may have conceptualized as difficult and to reframe it as a superpower. This intervention also invites nurture, as there will be healthy food that the caregiver and child might share together or feed to each other. This activity also translates well through telehealth—clinicians can have the session with the caregiver and child using the materials available in the client's kitchen.

TREATMENT GOALS:

- Explore emotions that are easy for the client (or each part of the dyad) to experience
- Project one difficult emotion onto a playful creation
- Identify the signals this emotion gives the client that action of some kind is needed
- Identify the actions that can be taken once the feeling is named

MATERIALS NEEDED:

- The book *How Are You Peeling? Foods with Moods* (Freymann & Elffers, 2004)*
- Fruits and vegetables
- Items to decorate the food characters—these could include other foods and/or craft supplies (fabric, yarn, etc.)
- Knife or cutting tool (only under the supervision of a Safe Boss)

DIRECTIONS:

1. Explain that part of being human is feeling lots of big feelings. Some of these are easy for us to feel and others we try to stuff down or ignore because we don't like having them.

2. Read the book *How Are You Peeling?* As you read, ask each participant to become curious about one emotion that they don't like feeling.

3. Once the client has identified a difficult emotion, invite them to create a food with this mood. The idea is to create a super-feeling fruit or vegetable. The sky is the limit. The client can choose a fruit or vegetable as the body, add dried beans or raisins as the eyes, use a knife to carve a mouth, and so on.

---

*There is a second book, *Fun with Foods*, that offers more variety in the food creation options, which can be used instead.

4. Encourage the client to make any superhero accessories (cape, mask, magic lasso, magic wand, etc.) that the fruit or vegetable might need to appropriately express the uncomfortable feeling.

5. Explore together the helpful information the feeling gives the client and name together the healthy actions the client can take when they feel this feeling.

⌐ 7.6 ⌐ FEELINGS SOUP

DESCRIPTION:

Clients with externalizing behaviors often lack the words to share their emotions verbally, so their feelings come out in their bodies. Emotions are also abstractions, and child clients can work with feelings more easily when physical representations of feelings can be held and kinesthetically manipulated. In this activity, clients will use colored gems to identify feelings and the quantity of each feeling in relation to a variety of events, creating a "feelings soup" for each event as they learn that multiple feelings can be experienced simultaneously.

TREATMENT GOALS:

- Help the client identify emotions and expand their feelings vocabulary

- Increase the client's understanding that multiple feelings can be present at the same time

MATERIALS NEEDED:

- A basket of glass gems in different colors
- Sticky notes or index cards

- A play pot and spoon
- Markers

DIRECTIONS:

1. Give the client the basket of colored gems and invite them to begin sorting them into piles by color. While their hands are busy sorting gems, explain the idea that a person can have several feelings at the same time in response to the same situation.

2. Help the client pair each colored gem pile with a feeling word and write it on an index card or sticky note next to the corresponding pile.

3. Describe an event—for example, a child named Johnny is having his first soccer game today after school—and decide together what emotions he may be feeling. He may be excited, nervous, and tired all at the same time. Engage the child in choosing handfuls of gems to represent how much of each feeling Johnny might have, and put them in the feelings soup pot.

4. Stir the soup and see how all the feelings exist together in the pot.

5. Once the client understands the premise of the exercise, you can create feelings soups for a variety of situations in the client's life. With young children, you can serve the soup in bowls and pretend to eat feelings soup together. You can also take pictures of each soup concoction, print them out, and put them together in a personalized cookbook of the client's feelings soups.

7.7 SECRET MESSAGES*

DESCRIPTION:

When a child is having difficulty sharing a feeling or expressing their thoughts and feelings on a topic, have them create a scribble picture. Children with big behaviors often have their emotions come out of their bodies instead of their mouths. This activity provides a nonverbal way to express their feelings and can be the start of creating a shared understanding. The scribble picture helps the child feel "heard," even without having to use words, while opening up an opportunity for further dialogue or processing.

TREATMENT GOALS:

- Provide the client with language for big feelings that are hard to express verbally

MATERIALS NEEDED:

- Paper
- Markers

DIRECTIONS:

1. Ask the client to scribble on a piece of paper without stopping for 30 seconds.

2. When they finish, tell the child that our brains sometimes share secret messages when it's hard for us to use words to communicate.

3. Using a different color, take the picture and trace a word out of the scribbles—specifically, a word that may relate to what the child may be experiencing (sad, mad, mom, school, etc.). Spoiler alert: You can basically make a scribble picture say anything.**

4. After identifying the word, have the child do another scribble picture, and see what words they can identify. Or they can identify another picture within the scribble, rather than words. If the child responds with some openness when you identify the word, you can move on from doing another scribble and have them draw a picture on the topic of the identified word.

---

*Created by Michelle Codington, MS, LMFT, RPT-S, CFPT.

**If the child's scribble truly cannot be made into a word, you can do your own scribble picture, and then identify a word (the same word you would have identified in their picture).

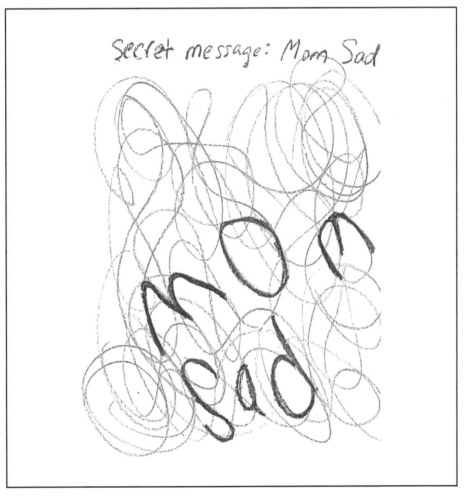

7.8 | REVEALING YOUR FEELINGS*

DESCRIPTION:

Since many clients avoid discussing distressing emotions, this technique was developed to facilitate emotional expression of "hidden" feelings. Using an "invisible" marker, the therapist and client take turns revealing the "hidden" feelings, which are then processed. This activity also works well with a group or family.

TREATMENT GOALS:

- Facilitate emotional expression
- Validate and normalize emotions
- Broaden the client's emotional vocabulary
- Identify coping strategies

MATERIALS NEEDED:

- Paper
- Color-changing markers
- Black marker

DIRECTIONS:

1. Prior to the session, draw various shapes (squares, circles, triangles, hearts, etc.) on the paper using a black marker. The shapes need to be large enough for feeling words to be written inside. Then, using the invisible marker from the package of color-changing markers, write various feeling words** inside the shapes.

2. During the session, have the players take turns coloring a shape with one of the colorful color-changing markers. Coloring in the shape will reveal the feeling that you previously wrote inside the shape with the invisible marker.

3. After the feeling has been revealed, ask the player to discuss a time they experienced that emotion.

4. Throughout the activity, take the opportunity to normalize and validate the emotions discussed by the client.

5. As an additional component, identify and discuss coping skills clients can use to manage emotional distress.

---

*Reprinted with permission from *Techniques-Techniques-Techniques: Play-Based Activities for Children, Adolescents, and Families* (Kenney-Noziska, 2008/2012).

**You can select specific emotions pertaining to the client's diagnosis, treatment plan, or treatment goals. For example, if the client is experiencing depression, you can select *depressed, sad,* and *upset* as three of the feelings to write inside the shapes. For an anxious child, you can choose the words *anxious, nervous,* and *worried.* The ability to prescriptively select specific emotions allows clinical discretion to ensure treatment goals are addressed.

VARIATION:

In some of the shapes, write the word *treat* instead of a feeling word, and have treats (e.g., candy or stickers) ready. When a player reveals this word, they can take a treat and discuss a feeling of their choice. The prospect of "winning" something during the course of the activity may lower clients' defenses, and it adds an additional component of playfulness to the technique.

| 7.9 | # STANDING IN IT TOGETHER

DESCRIPTION:

At the heart of caregiver co-regulation is *being with* the child through difficult emotions and working to organize their feelings at this time. Children with big behaviors sometimes have feelings that they can't interpret for themselves or don't feel safe to share with a caregiver. This intervention invites dyads to explore what it "feels like" (literally and figuratively) to stand in the big feeling together.

TREATMENT GOALS:

- Increase emotional literacy
- Expand the client's feelings vocabulary
- Increase the caregiver's ability to hold big feelings for the child

MATERIALS NEEDED:

- Different colors of construction paper, felt, or similar, cut into squares that are large enough for two people to stand on together (or, even better, liquid color floor tiles)

DIRECTIONS:

1. Explain to the client that some feelings are easier to feel than others. Happiness, for example, may be easier for us to feel than fear. However, being able to acknowledge and experience all our feelings and have our Safe Boss stick together with us through them is part of what helps us feel connected, and part of the function of a family.

2. Help the caregiver and child decide which color squares will represent each feeling.

3. Encourage each of them to step onto the different feelings and to identify a time that they have felt each of these feelings.

4. Ask which feeling they would like to stand in together. (It is likely to be a positive one, like happy, loving, or silly.)

5. Encourage the dyad to identify a feeling that is harder for them to share, and then have them step onto that feeling square together.

6. While they are standing in the feeling together, invite each of them to tell you how it feels to be in this together, and ask for any thoughts that have come up.*

---

*Some clients, particularly adoptive children, will think they'd rather be alone in the feeling. Sometimes this processing leads to a conversation about how hard it can be to be close to someone when you have a big feeling. Another question might be "What is your body telling you about being this close to your caregiver in this feeling?" If the client says they feel like they need more space, play around with the distance between the caregiver and child until both feel comfortable.

7.10 CHALK BOMBS*

DESCRIPTION:

Sometimes children have trouble expressing their feelings verbally, and the felt dysregulation often comes out in their bodies instead. This activity provides a kinesthetic, playful way to approach what may be a scary topic for children with big behaviors: emotions.

TREATMENT GOALS:

- Increase the client's ability to identify and express emotions
- Make the expression of emotions playful and fun
- Provide the client with an opportunity to relieve pent-up anger and/or anxiety
- Teach positive coping skills (specifically, deep-breathing skills)
- Allow self-expression to occur
- Open up dialogue for further processing

MATERIALS NEEDED:

- Chalk bombs
- *Feelings Chart* handout to help the client identify which feeling to talk about next if they get stuck (optional)

DIRECTIONS:

1. Bring the client outside and explain to them that these "bombs" are meant to be thrown at the sidewalk, driveway, or wall of a building (with permission).

2. Let them practice a few times throwing the bombs and seeing the chalk marks left behind.

3. Start with a simple and easy feeling, such as happy, and ask the client to describe a time when they were happy or to describe something that makes them happy. Then direct them to throw the bomb. You can ask them to show "how big" the feeling is, with the force of the throw/slam of the chalk bomb corresponding with how happy that event or thing made them.

4. After a few times of describing something that has made them happy, allow them to choose the next feeling and continue on. You can have them use a different color chalk bomb for each emotion—this has the added benefit of creating beautiful, multicolor art on the sidewalk or driveway. You can also incorporate breathing skills into the activity by having the client take a deep breath before throwing the chalk bomb.

*Created by Michelle Codington, MS, LMFT, RPT-S, CFPT.

FEELINGS CHART HANDOUT

 ANGRY

 BORED

 CONFIDENT

 **CONFUSED**

 DISAPPOINTED

 **EMBARRASSED**

 EXCITED

 FRUSTRATED

 GRUMPY

 GUILTY

 HAPPY

 HOPEFUL

 HUNGRY

 SAD

 SCARED

 SHY

 SICK

 **SLEEPY**

 **STRESSED**

 **WORRIED**

7.11 "PARTS OF ME" JOURNAL*

DESCRIPTION:

Children who have experienced a traumatic event may not have the language to express themselves. Increasing their emotional literacy can help them express how they feel toward themselves during and after a traumatic experience. This journal activity assists children in identifying their emotions around an experience and developing a journal that they can revisit when needed.

TREATMENT GOALS:

- Increase the client's emotional word bank
- Create and utilize expressive arts and journaling as a coping skill to express emotions
- Increase the client's knowledge of where emotion is present in the body

MATERIALS NEEDED:

- Multiple copies of the *"Parts of Me"* journal page (or other lined or blank paper)
- Construction paper
- Coloring utensils
- Stapler (or another way to bind the journal, such as a three-hole punch and a binder)
- *Feelings Chart* handout (from the *Chalk Bombs* activity [7.10])

DIRECTIONS:

Journal Creation

1. Invite the client to create a cover for the journal with construction paper.
2. Invite the client to create a list of rules or boundaries as the first page of the journal, such as "I only work on my journal with my therapist" or "I get to decide who sees my journal." Focus on giving the client permission to use the journal how they want to use it.
3. After the list of rules, include multiple journal pages and a back cover.
4. Bind the journal by stapling it along the left side.

Journal Entry

1. Provide the client with the *Feelings Chart* handout as a resource.
2. Invite the client to identify a situation to journal about. (They can choose any situation, difficult or fun, such as a trauma or a warm memory.)

---

*Created by Carmen Jimenez-Pride, LCSW, RPT-S.

3. Ask the client to pick feelings from the chart that they felt in response to the situation. Invite them to utilize the journal to write down their feelings and to identify where they felt each emotion in their body.

4. Then invite the client to assign each feeling a color and to fill in the figure on the journal page to show where they felt the feelings in their body.

VARIATION:

To expand this activity, you can invite the client to use a sand tray as they talk about the event and their feelings, then take a picture of their completed sand tray and glue it into the journal.

"PARTS OF ME" JOURNAL PAGE

Situation or memory: _____

_____

_____

_____

What I felt: _____

_____

_____

_____

Where I felt these feelings in my body:

Enhancing Social Skills
and Self-Esteem

Most clinicians have heard the phrase "children act bad when they feel bad." Regardless of the specific diagnosis, children act in distressing ways when they are in distress. They may blurt out hurtful things, grab toys from peers, or barge right into the center of a group of kids who are playing a game. Clients with big behaviors may also have trouble matching their volume to the setting, such as speaking loudly in the library when other students are reading quietly, or be unable to stop talking when they are supposed to be listening to a friend. Enough of these social infractions and they begin to experience rejection by their siblings or peers. They may also simultaneously get in trouble with their caregivers or teachers. These layers of discordant interactions lead these children to experience a loss of agency and a sense of helplessness related to making and keeping friends. Their self-esteem takes blow after blow, until they believe that nobody likes them and that nothing will change that fact.

Many children and teens have a deep sense of *badness* when they first enter treatment. Therefore, the activities in this chapter are intended to bring back the truth of the child's *goodness* to the client and their caregivers. These activities offer social skills practice, including giving and receiving positive affirmations, saying positive things about themselves and the situation, setting appropriate boundaries and respecting other people's boundaries, and taking turns and collaborating in play with peers. When working to build social skills with children, particularly those who are neurodivergent, be mindful of presenting these activities in an affirming and nonjudgmental way. Neurodivergent clients can find it especially challenging to read nonverbal cues like facial expression and tone of voice, so it is essential to practice reading and responding to social cues in friendly, nonjudgmental ways. With continued practice, children can increase their sense of agency and self-worth.

It may also be helpful to support children in deepening their own internal awareness of somatic body cues that occur in response to the presence of healthy and unhealthy boundaries in relation to others. That way, they can discern the presence of felt safety or toxicity in their relationships. This mind-body connection can support the development of personal agency and serve as a prompt to assert themselves if a boundary violation has been made. Practicing ways to make and keep healthy boundaries with others takes practice, and some of the exercises in this chapter support clients in setting boundaries and communicating those boundaries kindly, but clearly, to others.

FISHING FOR COMPLIMENTS

DESCRIPTION:

Clients with big behaviors such as impulsivity, anger escalations, or patterns of overresponding or underresponding in social situations may have trouble making and maintaining friendships. This sense of isolation can contribute to even more escalation. It is helpful for these children to practice discrete prosocial skill sets. This intervention helps clients learn and practice several ways of beginning interactions with a compliment. It's also a great game to use with groups and in family sessions.

TREATMENT GOALS:

- Enhance prosocial engagement
- Increase the client's ability to make positive verbalizations to others
- Enhance self-esteem

MATERIALS NEEDED:

- Tinfoil or shiny wrapping paper
- Multicolored Swedish Fish® (the assortment that includes red, orange, yellow, and green)
- Gummy worms
- Paper clips
- Colored paper
- Index cards

DIRECTIONS:

1. Place the shiny paper in the middle of the group of participants, and explain that this paper will be the fishing pond.

2. Explain to the participants that there are several kinds of compliments. Saying something kind to someone else can be a good way to start a conversation, and it makes both parties feel good.

3. Using four index cards, write one category of compliments on each card:

   - Physical attributes
   - Skills and abilities
   - Self-care
   - The way you treat others

4. Place these category cards at each of the four corners of the shiny paper.

5. Place enough Swedish Fish of each color in the middle of the pond.

6. Give each player a gummy worm and a paper clip. Have them each unfold the paper clip and stick one end through the gummy worm. This will represent the bait.

7. Each player then takes a turn catching a fish by spearing the protruding end of the paper clip into a Swedish Fish, and then gives a compliment to someone in the group. When a player receives a compliment, part of the game is trying to figure out which category of compliment it is. For example, if the giver of the compliment says, "I like your hair" or "You have a great smile" or "Cool shoes," the guesser would determine which of the four category cards describes that kind of compliment. (In this case, it would be physical attributes.)

8. Try to play until each person has gotten to practice giving each kind of compliment.

8.2 LEGO® COLLABORATION*

DESCRIPTION:

This play intervention is designed to help children address some specific social navigation needs they may be struggling with or wanting to improve. LEGO play is used to help children internalize their social navigation needs through an affirming play process.

TREATMENT GOALS:

- Address social navigation needs related to turn-taking
- Practice playing with another child in reciprocal interaction
- Practice completing a task with another person
- Increase comfort with working/playing with another person
- Increase perspective taking

MATERIALS NEEDED:

- A variety of LEGO bricks (60–80 pieces) or DUPLO® bricks (20–40 pieces)

DIRECTIONS:

1. Explain to the client that the two of you will be doing a play activity together that involves using the bricks and building something.

2. Take turns selecting one brick at a time from the pile, until the pile is gone and you each have an equal number of bricks.

3. Once the turn-taking and brick selection is complete, explain that each of you can now build whatever you want with the bricks you have. It can be something real or imagined, literal or abstract—there are no rules for what can be built with the bricks.

4. Once you both have finished your builds, take turns sharing about your builds—what you built and anything else you each want to share.

5. After the sharing, explain that you will now need to work together to combine your builds into one main build. Talk about what you would like to do and come together with a plan. Then join your two builds to form a new build. The joining process has no rules—bricks can be moved or changed, and the new build can be anything. The only guideline is that the two of you must work together.

6. Once the new build has been created, talk with the client about your creation and give it a name if they want. You can also help them reflect on the process of building individually versus building together. If there are any therapy goals you want to emphasize, this would be the time to highlight those (for example, reflecting on how you took turns and built something cool by working together).

---

*Created by Robert Jason Grant, EdD, LPC, RPT-S, ACAS.

BOUNDARY CATCHERS*

DESCRIPTION:

This activity provides the client with a developmentally appropriate rationale for the need for and importance of having healthy boundaries in relationships with others. Through the use of a physical object that concretizes the concept of boundaries, children can more easily understand the importance of communicating and reinforcing physical and emotional boundaries with others.

TREATMENT GOALS:

- Increase the client's understanding of boundaries and their importance in establishing and maintaining healthy, safe relationships

- Strengthen the client's understanding of and appreciation for the mind-body connection by deepening their awareness of their internal cues when their boundaries are or are not respected by others

- Empower the client to recognize and take appropriate action when a boundary violation has been made in a relationship context

- Encourage the client to make healthy choices and take responsibility for themselves by increasing their awareness of self-agency, personal responsibility, and personal influence

MATERIALS NEEDED:

- Suncatcher (plastic shape with black outline; available at most craft stores)

- Suncatcher paint

- String

DIRECTIONS:

1. Describe boundaries using a developmentally appropriate version of the following script:

   "*Boundaries* is a fancy word for how we know where to stop. It's where one thing ends and another thing begins. When you close the door to your bedroom while you are changing, you are telling people where to stop. You are setting a boundary. Boundaries help keep us safe. When we pull up to a stop sign, we stop. Otherwise, we could get into an accident. Once the boundary has been set, people usually stop. If they don't respect our boundaries, there are things we can do."

---

*Created by Eleah Hyatt, MA, LMFT, RPT.

2. After the client has gained a good understanding of the role and necessity of boundaries, introduce the suncatcher as a way to concretize the boundary concepts you've discussed. Invite the client to choose a blank suncatcher. Reflect on the many raised outlines that serve as boundaries in the art design. Discuss the importance of these different boundaries and how, together, they contribute to maintaining the essence of the design.

3. Next, invite the client to add suncatcher paint. As they work to carefully add the paint to the spaces inside the boundaries, discuss how the paint colors in each section are intended to remain within the bounds of that space.

> "There are times in life when we work really hard to set and hold good boundaries, just like I see you working to do right now as you fill in these spaces with paint. Slowing down as you fill these spaces with paint is a good reminder that boundary setting is a process that takes time and effort to learn. In order for us to have the healthiest and clearest relationships with friends and family, it is important that we learn how to respect one another's boundaries, even if they look different than our own."

Be especially intentional about reflecting on moments when paint may cross over a boundary and mix with another color.

> "Sometimes the process of learning how to set and hold good boundaries can become kind of messy, and boundaries can become crossed as we learn what is okay and what is not okay, just like this little bit of paint that spilled over this edge."

The point of this is not to correct the "oops" but to notice with the child how a boundary violation can affect the integrity of both spaces and, ultimately, the quality of the final product. This may also a good time to explore situations when a boundary crossing may need to be swiftly corrected, such as a boundary crossing affecting felt safety or a crossing that may have lasting impacts on a child's internal sense of self, thereby affecting the quality of the "final product" in an iatrogenic manner.

> "What changes do you notice in the spaces where this little bit of paint spilled over? Do you see a new color or cool paint design? How do you feel about what you see? Does it feel important to correct the boundary crossing or leave the new design as is?"

The final product is not "all" bad if the colors are all mixed together, but it can lessen the value of individual colors to the art piece as a whole. Or, the creation of the mixed colors can be reframed into a new, positive outcome. This can be applied to the concept of healthy relationships and the value of respecting boundaries, sticking together, and celebrating differences.

4. You can help the client problem-solve through the "oops" and identify ways to take action to correct the paint spillover as a way of reestablishing the boundary. You can then help the client apply this to a real-life situation where they may have felt a personal boundary was crossed and may need to advocate for themselves

by reasserting the boundary with the person who has been pushy, aggressive, disrespectful, or thoughtless toward them.

"Often when a boundary is crossed, people on both sides of the line can feel the change. Sometimes these boundary crossings need to be corrected quickly, like when someone says or does something to you that makes you feel unsafe or confused or when the boundary crossing changes how you feel about yourself in a negative way. Other times, the boundary crossing can turn out to be a helpful thing, like when you stretch your bravery to try something new or when you share a deeper feeling about yourself with a trusted friend. Those are examples of times when the original paint colors in both spaces change because of a spill, making your final product more beautiful and unique than before."

5. String can be attached to the final product so that it can be hung on a window. When the child sees the suncatcher, it can be a reminder of the beauty that can be found when we respect one another's differences while staying in relationship together. Similarly, it can symbolize transforming an unexpected relationship "oops" into a more authentic knowing and support of one another.

SOCIAL SOLAR SYSTEM

DESCRIPTION:

Clients with big behaviors can have conflict in many of their relationships or have a limited number of relationships due to the difficulties involved in remaining connected to others. This intervention can serve as an assessment of the number and quality of the social relationships that a client has with family and friends. Processing the intervention can help guide treatment planning around what sorts of relationships and what sorts of prosocial skills need to be supported.

TREATMENT GOALS:

- Assess the current constellation of family and friends who serve as social supports for the client
- Identify any gaps in the child's support network
- Explore the client's patterns of interaction that can make maintaining relationships difficult
- Identify goals for increasing the number or quality of relationships the client has

MATERIALS NEEDED:

- Black construction paper
- A chalk marker
- Stickers in the shapes of circles and stars

DIRECTIONS:

1. Explore what the client already knows about the stars and the planets.

2. Invite the client to choose a circle sticker to represent themselves as the sun, the center of the social solar system, in the middle of the black paper. Label this sticker with a chalk marker.

3. Invite the client to choose additional circle stickers (planets) and star stickers and to place them with varying degrees of proximity to the sun, depending on how close they feel to different people in their lives. If, for example, they feel really close to their mom, they can place a planet to represent their mom right next to the sun on the paper. If they have people in their lives with whom they feel distant, they may place these stickers on the edges of the paper, far away from the sun in the center.

4. If the client identifies a person with whom they have a conflictual relationship, explore further whether to bring that person closer to or father away from the sun. For example, if the client also experiences enjoyable times with the other person,

perhaps they need to figure out healthier ways to interact. However, if that person is an unhealthy influence, the answer may be separation.

5. Reflect on any patterns you and the client see emerging in their system. Use this assessment as a guide to treatment planning, collaboratively setting goals with the client for specific areas of growth in their social relationships.

8.5 FOLLOW THE LEADER—DRUMMING IN DYADS

DESCRIPTION:

An important aspect of co-regulation between caregiver and child is attunement. When children engage in big behaviors, there is often a lack of attunement to underlying cues in the dyad. Drumming can encourage increased attunement between the caregiver and child as they explore the notes and rhythms together. Drums made from the heads of propane tanks make beautiful sounds when struck and allow for eight different notes to be played. I encourage you to use a propane tank drum for this activity if possible.

TREATMENT GOALS:

- Enhance attunement between the client and caregiver
- Practice serve-and-return communication as both leader and follower
- Extend attention as patterns are repeated and lengthened

MATERIALS NEEDED:

- Drums—ideally, a propane tank drum or a xylophone (to allow multiple notes)
- Soft rubber mallets*

DIRECTIONS:

1. Introduce the caregiver and the client to the drum and give them each a mallet or a set of mallets.

2. Ask one partner to be the leader and create a pattern of three notes. Then invite the other partner to copy this pattern. Continue turn-taking and mirroring as patterns are extended. Increase the challenge as the dyad gains confidence.

3. Move into shared rhythms and patterns of drumming in which they both strike notes at the same time, attuning even more to each other.

4. Explore with the child first, and then the caregiver, how it felt to set the pattern and how it felt to follow the pattern. Emotions such as excitement, anxiety, frustration, and pride might emerge. Explore more deeply the roles each partner takes in daily life.

5. Ask the child, and then the caregiver, to give examples of moments of family life in which attunement was achieved and moments when they were out of rhythm with each other.

---

*You can purchase the mallets or make your own by drilling a small hole into a rubber ball, then hot gluing a wooden dowel into the hole. You could even invite the clients to create their own mallets in session.

8.6 SHARING YOUR TREASURES

DESCRIPTION:

Clients with big behaviors have often experienced a lot of negative or corrective feedback from their peers, caregivers, and teachers. These feedback loops may have negatively impacted their self-esteem. This intervention is aimed at helping clients rehearse their positive attributes while verbalizing statements of self-affirmation.

TREATMENT GOALS:

- Help the client identify their strengths or unique gifts
- Help the client verbalize positive self-statements

MATERIALS NEEDED:

- *Treasure Chest* template
- Markers or crayons
- Pad of sticky notes
- A full-sized treasure chest with play gems
- Make-your-own treasure chest kit (small wooden or cardboard chest and decorations such as paints)

DIRECTIONS:

1. Explain to the client that we all have beautiful things inside of us—sometimes they are just buried under our worries, anger, and stress.

2. Invite the client to play with the actual treasure chest, letting the child kinesthetically engage with the materials while talking about divers who uncover treasure chests.

3. Ask them to imagine themselves as a treasure chest. Using the *Treasure Chest* template, invite them to write one skill or ability (something in which they excel) on each of the coins and one positive character trait on each of the gems.

4. If they have trouble identifying their strengths, invite their caregiver to participate, or offer your own insights regarding the client's strengths.

5. Using the make-your-own treasure chest materials, invite the client to create a personalized treasure chest. Offer the sticky note pad to the client's family and ask them to write down strengths, skills, abilities, and kindnesses they see in the client and to place them in the treasure chest. Ask the caregiver to identify at least one per day, between that session and the next.

6. During the next session, open the treasure chest and invite the client and their caregiver to read the positive statements out loud.

VARIATION FOR TELEHEALTH:

Let the client choose an online game that allows the player to accrue treasure as part of moving from level to level. Have the client identify a positive self-attribute each time they accrue treasure in the game.

TREASURE CHEST TEMPLATE

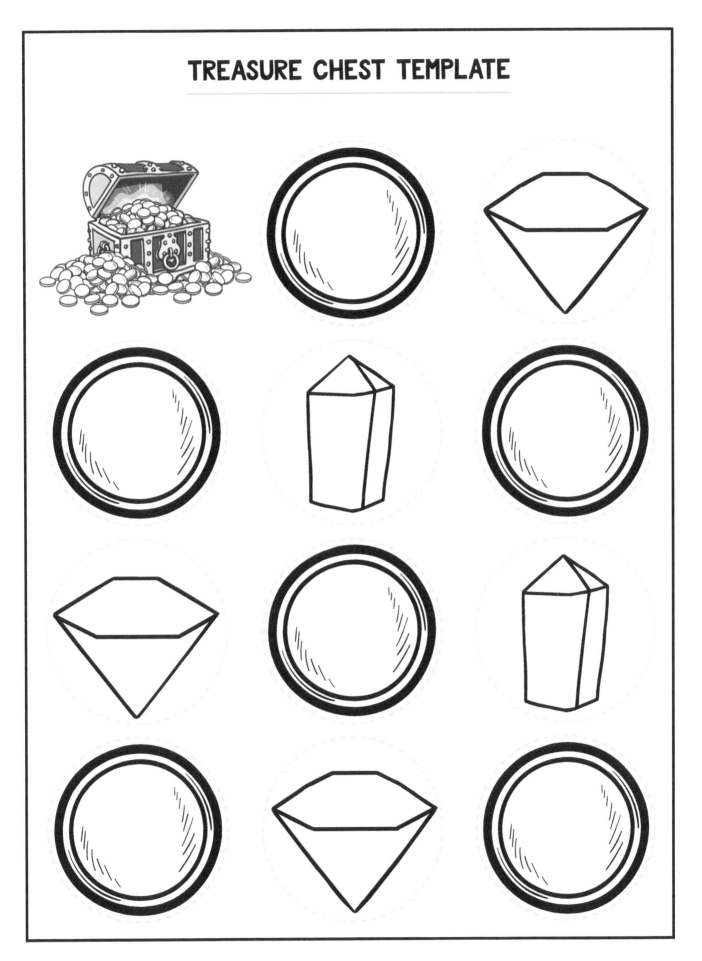

CLAY ROSES

DESCRIPTION:

Children with low self-esteem need more positive affirmations from their caregivers than those with healthy self-esteem. This intervention offers a kinesthetically grounded way for children or teens with low self-esteem to explore their positive traits and have their worth affirmed by both the therapist and the caregiver, as the client practices affirming themselves and others.

TREATMENT GOALS:

- Enhance delight between the caregiver and child
- Assist the client and their caregiver in offering positive affirmations to each other
- Provide a concrete reminder of the positive affirmations

MATERIALS NEEDED:

- Modeling clay in multiple colors
- A hard surface

DIRECTIONS:

1. Invite the caregiver and child to sit together in front of a table or a hard surface placed on the floor.

2. Offer the selection of modeling clay to the dyad and take some for yourself.

3. Show them how to pull off a small piece of clay from the larger piece, roll it into a ball between their hands, and then smash it onto the hard surface until it looks like a pancake about the size of a quarter.*

4. Repeat this process, placing the next quarter-sized flat circle of clay next to and partially on top of the first (so they overlap slightly).

5. Have the dyad continue adding pieces to the overlapping chain. For each piece of clay they add to the chain, the caregiver or child should make one positive affirmation of the other.

6. Once the chain is complete (this usually requires 7–10 pieces), begin carefully rolling it up from left to right.

7. As the pieces are rolled together, they begin to take the form of a rose. This can serve as a reminder that as family members intentionally affirm each other, beautiful things are created.

---

*As children press their fingerprints into the clay or press the ball of clay flat with the palm of their hands, unique imprints can be left behind. This can become another richly therapeutic way to talk about the unique beauty in each of us and the importance of naming the uniqueness we see in one another.

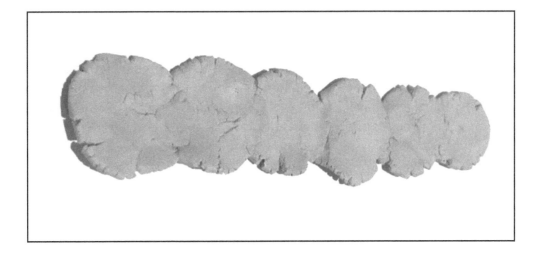

MAGNIFY THE FEEL-GOODS

DESCRIPTION:

Children who struggle with dysregulation may experience more negative interactions with people than their typically developing peers. In turn, they may have amplified the negative messages of others and have trouble believing positive things about themselves. This intervention acknowledges the amplification effect and then uses it to amplify positive qualities of the child in a playful way.

TREATMENT GOALS:

- Identify negative self-talk
- Assist the client in identifying positive self-talk
- Practice amplifying the positive self-talk

MATERIALS NEEDED:

- Magnifying glass
- Tiny toy lizard or spider
- *Magnify the Feel-Goods* handout
- Several blank pieces of paper and a writing utensil

DIRECTIONS:

1. Ask the client to identify one negative self-talk statement that feels really big to them. It may frequently intrude on their performance, their thoughts, or their time with friends. Write down this statement in large print on a piece of paper.

2. Offer the client the magnifying glass. Have them look at the tiny toy lizard using just their eyes, and then have them look at the lizard using the magnifying glass. It looks much more threatening because it has been magnified.

3. Identify or craft a positive self-talk statement that can combat or replace the negative one. Write this in very small print on a separate piece of paper.

4. Have the client practice using the magnifying glass to make the positive replacement larger and easier to read.

5. Reflect on real-life practices that can help the client rehearse the positive self-talk.

6. On the *Magnify the Feel-Goods* handout, write the positive self-talk statement in the magnifying glass, and write down any strategies that will help the client practice the new self-talk. Identifying specific times of day to repeat the mantra (e.g., for two minutes while washing their hair) might be helpful.

MAGNIFY THE FEEL-GOODS HANDOUT

In the middle of the magnifying glass, write down one positive self-talk statement that helps you feel good. Then on the three lines provided, think of strategies you can use to practice this new self-talk.

_____

_____

_____

SAND TRAY CIRCLES

DESCRIPTION:

Clients who engage in big behaviors are less likely to experience positive interactions with their peers. They are more likely to develop low self-esteem and to have a hard time keeping the positive voices in their lives at the forefront of their heads and hearts. This activity offers a circle of symbols to remind clients of the people in their lives who say kind things that help build their self-esteem.

TREATMENT GOALS:

- Enhance the client's sense of positive community
- Amplify the voices of people in the client's life who speak positively to them

MATERIALS NEEDED:

- Sand tray
- Sand tray miniatures

DIRECTIONS:

1. Explain to the client that when it is hard for us to feel good about ourselves, it can be valuable to remember the kind, encouraging things that others in our lives believe about us.

2. Invite the client to choose at least four symbols to represent positive words others have spoken to them. These are people who have helped them grow or who have said nice things to or about them. Invite them to place these symbols in the shape of a circle in the sand tray.

3. Then ask the client to choose a symbol to represent themselves and have them place it in the middle of this circle of symbols.

4. Help the client imagine being surrounded by these amplified positive voices. Help them notice how their body feels in the middle of the circle. If you are trained in EMDR, this would be worth further installing with bilateral stimulation.

5. Take a picture of the sand tray, print it for the client, and ask them to keep it in a school binder or in another readily accessible place for them to use when they are feeling low.

MY PAMPERING PIZZA

DESCRIPTION:

Clients with big behaviors often do not pay enough attention to their self-care needs until they are far outside their optimal arousal windows. This can result in giant escalations or shutting-down behaviors in which the client overresponds or underresponds in situations that would normally be dealt with in a much more regulated way. This intervention encourages clients to articulate the kinds of activities that will keep them inside their window of tolerance in six distinct areas of self-care.

TREATMENT GOALS:

- Identify self-care practices that keep the client within their window of tolerance
- Playfully practice engaging in self-care outside of session

MATERIALS NEEDED:

- *My Pampering Pizza* template
- Modeling clay (in colors that can represent a pizza)

DIRECTIONS:

1. Introduce the idea of self-care as one important tool for staying within your window of tolerance for stress. This is especially important if you are working with the caregiver, as their self-care practices will directly affect their ability to care for the child with big behaviors.

2. Offer the *My Pampering Pizza* template. With young children, use modeling clay to create a concrete pampering pizza.

3. Identify at least one behavior in each of the categories to represent a self-care practice. Here are some examples:

   - **Emotional:** Read a book that makes you laugh, share something that makes you sad with your caregiver, let a friend help you with a big feeling
   - **Spiritual:** Write in your journal, walk in nature, pray, meditate
   - **Social:** Invite a friend over, call a friend, attend a youth group, join a club
   - **Mental:** Read a challenging book, divide studying times into several nights, think nice thoughts about yourself
   - **Physical:** Exercise, take a bubble bath, ride a bike, do yoga
   - **Basic needs:** Eat fruits and vegetable, have a protein rich-snack every two hours, stay hydrated, get eight hours of sleep each night

4. For a specified period of time, check in regularly to see how many of the self-care tasks have been prioritized.

MY PAMPERING PIZZA TEMPLATE

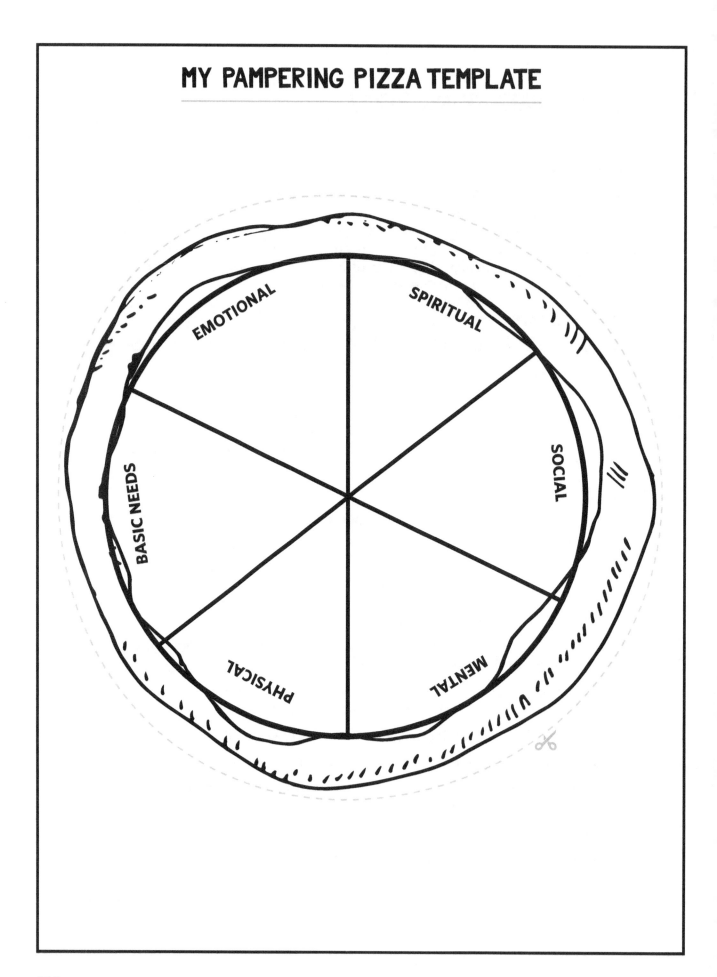

8.11 PUTTING A POSITIVE SPIN ON IT

DESCRIPTION:

Clients who have endured lots of correction because of big behaviors may have a harder time than their peers believing good things about themselves. This intervention offers a playful way for children to articulate negative self-talk, create positive self-talk statements, and practice verbalizing the replacement talk to amplify their self-esteem.

TREATMENT GOALS:

- Identify negative self-talk and develop alternate positive replacement statements
- Pair repetition of thought stopping and thought replacement with kinesthetic engagement and verbalization to enhance practice

MATERIALS NEEDED:

- A variety of spinning tops
- *Putting a Positive Spin on It* template
- Blank piece of paper
- Writing utensil

DIRECTIONS:

1. Help the client identify negative self-talk that leads up to behavioral outbursts or withdrawal from others.

2. Identify or craft positive self-talk statements the client can use when the negative thoughts start to play in their mind. Write these inside the spinning tops on the *Putting a Positive Spin on It* template.

3. Offer a variety of novel spinning tops. (Having a variety of shapes, colors, and materials will enhance the child's interest and increase the number of times they will practice.)

4. Write the negative self-talk statement on a piece of paper and use this as the launching point for the spinning top.

5. Have the client repeat the positive self-talk out loud on a loop for as long as the top spins. The top is unlikely to stay on the piece of paper the whole time it is spinning, and if it ends up away from the paper, you can comment on how practicing our positive self-talk helps distance us from the thoughts that make us feel bad.

PUTTING A POSITIVE SPIN ON IT TEMPLATE

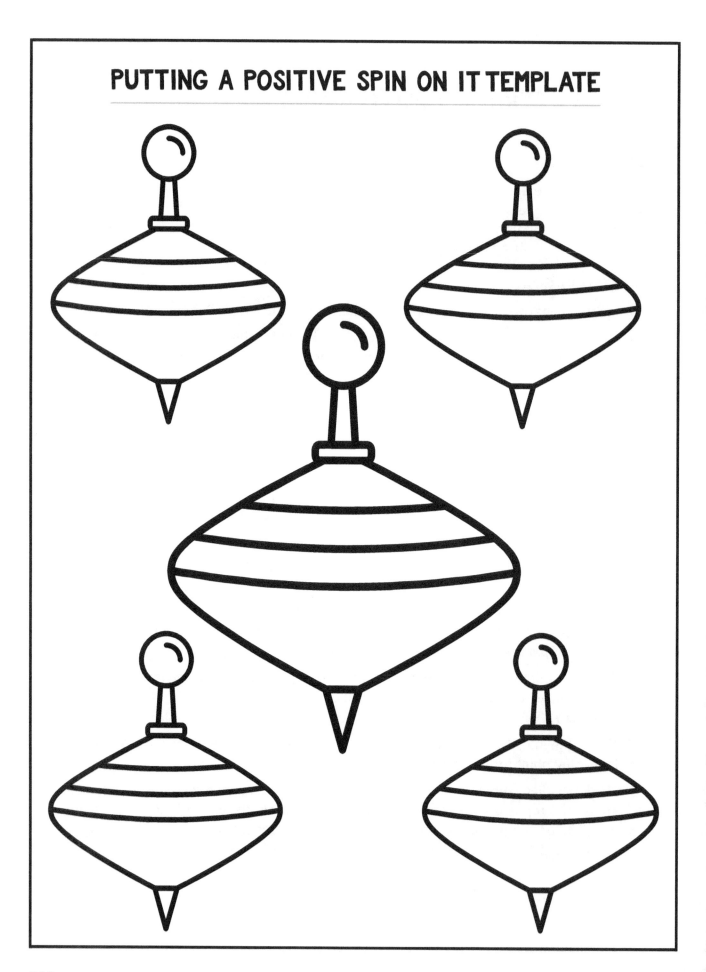

nine

Addressing the Thought Life

Children with big behaviors may need a lot of therapeutic support to become curious about their thought life and to understand how to change it. Since children with big behaviors are often doers and feelers first—causing them to bypass the thought life in moments of intense stress—it is important to start this part of the therapeutic process with psychoeducation about the cognitive triad (the relationship between our thoughts, emotions, and behaviors). Once clients realize that our thoughts, emotions, and behaviors are all connected, they can better understand how changing our thoughts can result in a subsequent change to how we feel and behave.

In addition, children with big behaviors need help identifying cognitive distortions, which can take the form of negative self-talk ("I'm stupid," "I'll never learn how to do this"), irrational thoughts that focus on the worst-case scenario ("What if the roof caves in?" "What if the plane crashes?"), or false attributions related to a specific event ("It's all my fault"). False attributions are especially important to explore when a client has experienced trauma. Trauma survivors often carry a set of beliefs that center on what they didn't do, should have done, or could have done during the trauma. For example, a teenage client who was sexually assaulted in her school parking lot might believe, "It happened because I wore a short skirt." The false responsibility that accompanies these statements causes clients to feel like they could have had some control over what happened.

The first step in shifting cognitions is identifying these various types of thinking. When working with children, we often ask them to verbalize the cognitive distortion while pairing it with a kinesthetic movement. For example, a child may say out loud, "I'm stupid" while ripping up a piece of paper on which this negative thought is written. Erasers, fire extinguishers, and Zen artist boards all offer concrete and playful ways for children to make their troubling thoughts disappear. For children with false attributions, interventions that place the blame squarely back on the perpetrator can be helpful when dealing with these types of cognitive distortions.

Another necessary component of treatment is to craft replacement statements, in which negative cognitions are countered with a positive cognition. However, coming up with replacement thoughts needs to be nuanced. An effective replacement thought is not simply the opposite of the ingrained negative self-talk. For example, a child who thinks, "I am stupid" is unlikely to feel soothed by a replacement like "I am brilliant" if they make C's and D's after studying hard for assignments. Clients must be able to own the replacement thoughts in order for them to be reliably useful. In this example, the client could identify one class in which they excel and say, "I am really good at math," or they could highlight a different kind of intelligence, like "I am super good at soccer." Thought work is a collaborative process between the therapist and client that often requires the support of caregivers in reinforcing new thinking patterns.

In addition to replacement thoughts, you can also work with children to identify "boss back" talk, which can be any set of words that the client uses to feel strong, competent, and powerful in relation to the cognitive distortion. Boss back talk is different from a simple cognitive replacement in that it externalizes the negative cognitions—in a form such as a barrage of balls or a mistake snake—to which the child can talk back like a boss. For example, let's assume a child has the following cognitive distortion: "She won't come back." Here, a positive replacement thought would simply be "She will come back," whereas with boss back talk, the child would imagine talking back to the figure representing the cognitive distortion by saying, "You're a liar!" or "I don't have to listen to you!" You can first practice boss back talk on paper and then practice it in full-body ways with clients.

Both boss back talk and cognitive replacement are empowering and useful ways to address the thought life with young clients. The interventions in this chapter will give you a multitude of ways to make this cognitive shift work fun and playful for your clients.

INNER CRITIC

DESCRIPTION:

Clients who engage in big behaviors often have an inner critic who takes over and begins to create shame in ways that impact (1) the onset of the big behaviors, (2) what the child communicates during the big behaviors, and (3) the self-loathing that can show up after their de-escalation. However, children can have difficulty dealing with abstract concepts like shame. This activity externalizes the shame, creating a three-dimensional representation of the inner critic.

TREATMENT GOALS:

- Externalize the negative self-talk related to the client's big behaviors
- Normalize the layering effect that can happen when a client becomes dysregulated and later experiences shame related to the acting out behaviors

MATERIALS NEEDED:

- Paper lunch bags, empty tissue boxes, or other items to form the body of the inner critic
- Pipe cleaners, googly eyes, colorful paper, and other decorations
- Scissors
- Glue
- Any other tools required for the materials selected

DIRECTIONS:

1. Explain to the client that we all have negative self-talk. When our negative self-talk gets really loud, we have trouble making good decisions and doing things to repair any relationship ruptures that may have occurred. For example, in the wake of an acting out episode, we might experience so much shame that we decide to pretend the episode never happened instead of repairing our relationship with the person or people we hurt.

2. Explain that the client will be creating an "inner critic." They might use a paper bag to make a puppet or use a box to form the critic's body. Then allow them to decorate the critic using their imagination and the materials available.

3. Once the inner critic has been created, help the client externalize their negative self-talk by identifying statements that the inner critic amplifies when acting out behavior has occurred.

4. Explain that the first step in self-regulating and being able to make repairs in relationships involves acknowledging that the shame or inner critic is present. You must first notice the troubling thought before you can counteract it with adaptive self-talk.

5. To help the client create this path for repair, follow this activity with the *Inner Kindness* activity (9.2).

9.2 | INNER KINDNESS

DESCRIPTION:

Children with big behaviors may benefit from a concretized version of nurture and repair. The client may have encoded significant judgment from the comments of peers and caregivers in the wake of their outbursts. This intervention is meant to be used after the *Inner Critic* activity (9.1). It will help the client surround the inner critic with comfort and create a path for repair.

TREATMENT GOALS:

- Acknowledge the shame or guilt that may be present in the wake of an acting out episode

- Become curious about what the most compassionate, mature part of themselves would say to the guilty or shamed part

- Help the client concretize a form of self-compassion

MATERIALS NEEDED:

- The *Inner Critic* model created in the previous activity (9.1)

- Art supplies and/or elements from nature that can be used to represent kindness

DIRECTIONS:

1. Become curious with the client about what their core self would say to the inner critic and what the most compassionate part of themselves would say to the client. If this is difficult for the client, you may need to identify an attachment figure whom they trust and have that person represent the client's compassionate voice. Or you may need to use your own voice with the client if they do not have healthy enough attachment figures.

2. Become curious about what the inner critic needs to still feel loved and accepted. Invite the client to create symbols with the art or nature materials to represent these kindness communications. Have the client place these items around the inner critic.

3. Help the client notice what it feels like to have the inner critic surrounded by kindness and compassion.

4. Wonder out loud if the client can now find a path toward making repair with whomever they hurt in their acting out episode.

5. If possible, help the client build a concrete bridge from the inner critic, through the kindness, to repair with whomever needs it.

9.3 WORRIES AND A ZEN ARTIST BOARD

DESCRIPTION:

Some clients with big behaviors feel so shamed by their negative self-talk (or by the trauma they endured) that they are unable to create a lasting representation of the trauma or the resulting negative self-talk. However, as the neuroception of safety grows with you, their clinician, they may risk sharing a glimpse of it. For this reason, it is important to have a way the client can show you "what happened," but then it needs to disappear, or be erasable, so that no concrete representation remains. This intervention offers such a path.

TREATMENT GOALS:

- Identify current negative self-talk, worry thoughts, or glimpses of the trauma
- Craft positive statements to replace the negative self-talk
- Engage in verbal rehearsal of positive self-talk

MATERIALS NEEDED:

- Zen artist board (or other water drawing board)
- Two soft-tipped paintbrushes (one that makes thin strokes and one that makes wide strokes)
- Water

DIRECTIONS:

1. This intervention is especially useful for children with overwhelming anxiety, anger, or low self-esteem. Help the client identify worry thoughts, angry thoughts, or negative self-talk, depending on the treatment need.

2. Invite the client to write one of the troublesome thoughts on the Zen artist board using the thin-tipped paintbrush and water.

3. Explain that eventually the thought will disappear on its own. The client may want to set a timer to see how long it takes the thought to evaporate naturally.

4. Then help the client to craft a positive replacement thought.

5. Next, rewrite the negative cognition on the board, and invite the client to use the wider brush to paint back and forth over the troublesome thought with more water—moving from one end of the Zen artist board to the other and back—while verbalizing the positive thought multiple times. The troubling thought is absorbed by the repetitive practice with the helpful thought.

6. This pattern can be repeated using another troubling thought once the Zen artist board has fully dried from the first round.

9.4 | THE CHEWING-IT-UP BRAIN

DESCRIPTION:

Clients who exhibit big behaviors as a response to trauma may need help leaching the emotional toxicity out of the trauma. When clients are introduced to the idea of trauma processing, one helpful metaphor compares trauma to the feeling of having overeaten. This intervention helps clients better understand that trauma has to be digested over time. If you are a fully trained and authorized practitioner of EMDR, this metaphor is helpful with that work as well (Gomez, 2007). This intervention should only be used after deep rapport and the neuroception of safety have been established with the client.

TREATMENT GOALS:

- Help the client identify negative self-talk statements
- Identify more positive, helpful replacements for these cognitive distortions
- Practice replacing the negative thoughts with the positive ones

MATERIALS NEEDED:

- A puppet or toy model of a brain
- Sticky notes or other small strips of paper
- Writing utensil

DIRECTIONS:

1. Explain the process by which trauma may get metabolized as we face it, bit by bit. Use the "chewing-it-up brain"—a brain with teeth—as a metaphor for trauma processing. You can use the following script:

   "Have you ever eaten so much at a meal that you felt uncomfortably full? Then your stomach acids get busy breaking down the meal into nutrients that it will absorb into your body and waste that will be expelled through pee and poop. Trauma is like that: There are parts of the story we want to keep, but all the toxic fallout that's bad for you, we want to help your body chew up and get rid of."

   Ask the client to identify negative self-talk statements they have. These may be statements like "It's all your fault. You deserved it. You are damaged goods." Write these statements on sticky notes and pretend to feed them to the traumatized brain.

2. Thought by thought, slip of paper by slip of paper, help the client craft positive replacement statements. This can be especially important in the case of false attributions. When a client blames themselves for hurt that occurred during abuse, it is helpful to have them practice statements that reframe the responsibility as resting firmly with the perpetrator's choices.

3. Pretend to have the brain ingest the new thoughts, and reflect on how believing these replacement thoughts may change the client's approach to certain situations and relationships.

9.5 | LOSE THE BRUISE

DESCRIPTION:

Clients who are easily kicked outside their window of tolerance can have negative self-talk as well as rigid thinking patterns and polarizing or catastrophizing thoughts. They also have trouble slowing down enough to identify these negative cognitions. This intervention helps children and teens address their thought life, stopping and replacing harmful thoughts with helpful thoughts while rehearsing through full-body, kinesthetic engagement.

TREATMENT GOALS:

- Identify irrational thoughts, negative self-talk, or false attributions related to trauma

- Practice replacing the cognitive distortions with positive replacement statements

- Pair repetition of thought stopping and thought replacement with kinesthetic engagement and verbalization to enhance empowerment

MATERIALS NEEDED:

- *Thought Brain* and *Sword and Shield* templates

- Toy sword and shield

- Small balls that look like they have been hurt (such as Hacky Sacks with bandages)

DIRECTIONS:

1. Introduce the *Thought Brain* template and help the client identify cognitive distortions related to their treatment goals. These might be anxious thoughts, thoughts that induce anger, depressive thoughts, negative self-talk, or in the case of abuse, lies that the client may have been told by the perpetrator that are still troublesome. Write those thoughts on the lines by the brain labeled Stressful Thoughts.

2. Then help the client identify positive replacement thoughts, boss back talk, or a combination of both. Write these on the lines by the brain labeled Strong and Soothing Thoughts.

3. Explain that the balls represent the hurtful thoughts, while the sword and shield represent the positive statements that the client can use to push away the hurtful thoughts.

4. Give the client the toy sword and the shield, and explain that you will throw the balls at the client while saying the negative self-talk out loud. Their job is to make sure the balls don't hit them (they can use the shield to deflect them or the sword to bat them

220

away) while they verbalize their positive replacement statements or their boss back talk.*

5. Help the client reflect on which thoughts feel most empowering, and write these down on the *Sword and Shield* template.

VARIATION:

Read the "Daniel the Dragon Slayer" story (Goodyear-Brown, 2021) to set up this activity, and use a dragon puppet to voice the negative cognitions before you throw the balls.

---

*Once children get their bodies involved in the cognitive processes of thought stopping and thought replacement, they often begin to generate additional thoughts. Be sure to add these to the *Thought Brain* handout. Clients who begin in a constricted posture can be encouraged to get louder and more assertive with their boss back talk as they deflect the balls.

THOUGHT BRAIN TEMPLATE

STRESSFUL THOUGHTS

STRONG AND SOOTHING THOUGHTS

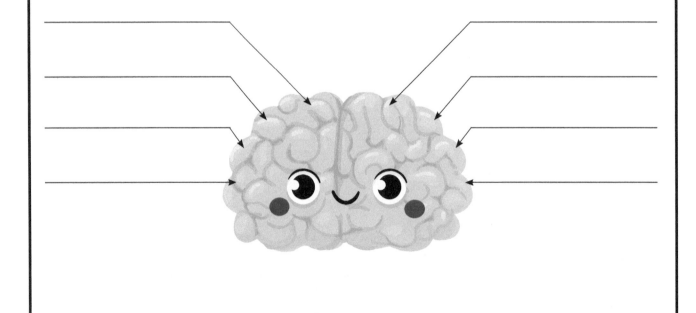

SWORD AND SHIELD TEMPLATE

HELPFUL THOUGHTS*

DESCRIPTION:

Children with big behaviors often need help identifying unhelpful thoughts and better understanding how these thoughts affect their feelings and behaviors. These clients also need help identifying or crafting helpful thoughts and lots of practice replacing one with the other. This activity offers an exploration of these concepts in a full-body way.

TREATMENT GOALS:

- Help the client articulate an understanding of the cognitive triangle (the connection between thoughts, feelings, and behaviors)
- Identify how changing thoughts can change feelings, body sensations, and behaviors
- Replace maladaptive thoughts with more adaptive thoughts

MATERIALS NEEDED:

- Three sheets of paper
- Masking tape or string

DIRECTIONS:

1. Write the word *thoughts* in large block letters on one sheet of paper, *feelings/ body sensations* on the second, and *behaviors* on the third. Place these in the shape of an equilateral triangle on the floor, with thoughts at the top corner, feelings/ body sensations at the bottom-right corner (about six feet away from thoughts), and behaviors at the bottom-left corner (about six feet away from feelings/body sensations).

2. Connect the three sheets of paper using masking tape or string to form the outline of a triangle on the floor.

3. Explain to the client that they will be learning how to change unhelpful thoughts to helpful thoughts by noticing how thoughts, feelings/body sensations, and behaviors are all connected. Talk about an example to help the client understand this connection. For instance:

   a. "Let's say you're afraid of spiders. You see a creepy-crawly spider on the floor. Your thoughts in the situation are: 'The spider is so creepy! It may crawl on me and that would be even creepier!' Thinking this makes you feel scared and yucky. The scared, yucky feelings make your heart pound faster and your body get tight and sweaty. Then you jump up on the chair so the creepy-crawly spider can't crawl on you!"

---

*Reprinted with permission from *Assessment and Treatment Activities for Children, Adolescents, and Families: Practitioners Share Their Most Effective Techniques* (Lowenstein, 2008).

b. After explaining this to the client, walk to the word *thoughts* at the top corner of the triangle. Repeat out loud the thoughts you have when you see the spider: "The spider is so creepy! It may crawl on me and that would be even creepier!"

c. Walk to the words *feelings/body sensations* at the bottom-right corner of the triangle. Repeat out loud your feelings and body sensations in this imagined situation: "scared, yucky, heart pounding faster, body tight, and sweaty."

d. Walk to the word *behaviors* at the bottom-left corner of the triangle. Repeat out loud your behaviors in this situation: "jump up on the chair."

e. Next, explain to the client how changing thoughts can change the entire cognitive triangle: "Thinking a different thought can change how we feel and behave. When you see a spider and you change the thought to 'It's just a tiny, harmless little thing; it can't hurt me,' then you feel calm and safe, and you are able to sit calmly in the chair."

f. Once you explain this to the client, walk to the word *thoughts* at the top corner of the triangle. Repeat out loud your thoughts this time when you see the spider: "It's just a tiny, harmless little thing; it can't hurt me."

g. Walk to the words *feelings/body sensations* at the bottom-right corner of the triangle. Repeat out loud your feelings and body sensations if you were to see the spider this time: "calm and safe, relaxed body."

h. Walk to the word *behaviors* at the bottom-left corner of the triangle. Repeat out loud your behaviors this time in this situation: "able to sit calmly in the chair."

4. Explore with the client differences in the way they feel and act when guided by different kinds of thoughts.

5. Identify the unhelpful thoughts with which the client struggles. Generate helpful thoughts and take turns walking the cognitive triangle with each of these.

9.7 PICK IT UP OR LAY IT DOWN?

DESCRIPTION:

Clients with big behaviors will sometimes blame their acting out on others: "Well, if he hadn't rolled his eyes at me, I wouldn't have hit him" or "She just made me so mad, I had to yell at her." This activity is meant to slow down the process of placing responsibility and pair it with a novel stimulus to help clients begin taking ownership for their choices and actions.

TREATMENT GOALS:

- Assist the client in accepting responsibility for their actions and behaviors
- Let go of false responsibility or shame related to the choices of others

MATERIALS NEEDED:

- Grab It Claw toy (or another gripper/grabber toy)
- *Pick It Up, Lay It Down* handout
- Scissors

DIRECTIONS:

1. Introduce the client to the toy. Let them practice grabbing things in the environment around them.

2. Then offer the *Pick It Up, Lay It Down* handout. Explain that we all make mistakes sometimes, but shame can keep us from accepting responsibility for hurtful things we may have done. There is freedom in owning your choice and simply saying, "I did it; I'm sorry" or "I made a mistake; I'll know for next time."

3. We can also be carrying things—responsibilities or burdens—that are not ours to carry. A child may believe, for example, that their parents got divorced because they fought with their siblings.

4. Help the client write down actions or behaviors that are theirs to "pick up" (theirs to own), and other behaviors or choices that need to be laid down.

5. Cut out the individual cards, shuffle them, and lay them face down. As the client picks up each choice, they decide which ones they keep (take responsibility for) and which ones they release. The second set can be released directly into a recycling bin if the client prefers.

6. Explore what it feels like for the client to take ownership for their choices and to let go of false responsibility.

PICK IT UP, LAY IT DOWN HANDOUT

On each card, write down actions or behaviors that are yours to "pick up" (yours to own), and other behaviors or choices that need to be laid down.

Pick It Up...

| Yep! I did it. | Yep! I did it. | Sorry, my mistake. | Sorry, my mistake. |

Lay It Down...

| Not mine to carry. | Not mine to carry. | They chose... It's not my fault. | They chose... It's not my fault. |

9.8 THE RECYCLER AND THE SHREDDER*

DESCRIPTION:

Clients with big behaviors are often caught in a loop of negative self-talk or other irrational thoughts. They push these thoughts down as long as possible, but the outgrowth of these cognitive distortions—as we apply the cognitive triad of thinking, feeling, and doing—is to eventually act out or act in. This intervention gives clients a metaphor for looping cognitions and an experience of chewing them up and being free of them.

TREATMENT GOALS:

- Provide opportunities for the client to express difficult emotions (e.g., fear, anger, hurt)
- Provide the client with a sense of power and control
- Identify cognitive distortions and craft positive replacement statements
- Help the client experience empowerment over their thought life by replacing distortions

MATERIALS NEEDED:

- Toy (or small) recycling bin
- Paper
- Writing utensil
- Miniature hand crank paper shredder (optional)

DIRECTIONS:

1. Provide the client with the recycling bin. Explain that we all have some troubling thoughts: thoughts that make us feel bad about ourselves, thoughts that make us angrier and more vengeful with others, and thoughts that make us more depressed or anxious. The ones that make us feel the worst can sometimes play over and over again in our minds. We try to throw the thought away, but it's like it goes in the recycling bin, and eventually we pull it back out.

2. Invite the client to write down any negative cognitions that loop this way.

3. Starting with the most troubling cognitive distortion, ask the client to create a positive replacement statement—one that, when they think it, helps them feel better about themselves or more regulated.

4. Instruct the client to shred the negative cognition, and have them repeat the positive replacement statement out loud while they do so. Clients tend to enjoy this part. They can either do it by hand or use the optional mini paper shredder. The kinesthetic involvement adds a layer to the intervention by allowing the client to experience the negative thought being changed into paper scraps.

5. Invite the client to throw these scraps into an actual trash can.

---

*Created by Michelle Codington, MS, LMFT, RPT-S, CFPT, and Tonya Haynes, MMFT.

9.9 RIGID ROB/FLEXIBLE FRED

DESCRIPTION:

Clients with big behaviors—especially those who carry diagnoses of ADHD, ODD, or OCD, or have significant trauma in their histories—tend to engage in rigid thinking patterns more than their peers. They have trouble with flexibility, believing that things *must* be a certain way. This rigidity often springs from underlying anxiety, but it is ultimately self-sabotaging because when they can't "go with the flow," bigger behaviors occur.

TREATMENT GOALS:

- Teach the MOANS acronym
- Identify rigid thinking patterns
- Identify words that combat the MOANS
- Pair rigid thinking words with flexible words
- Practice flexible thinking

MATERIALS NEEDED:

- *Rigid Rob* and *Flexible Fred* templates
- Two copies of the *Rigid/Flexible Thinking Hats* template
- Paper
- Pen
- Scissors
- Clothespins and clothesline/string (or magnets and a magnetic board)

DIRECTIONS:

1. Introduce the client to Rigid Rob (a robot with very defined rules about everything) and Flexible Fred (a Gumby-type creature who can go with the flow).

2. Teach the MOANS acronym, which is a set of words that create rigid thinking patterns when we use them:

    M   Must

    O   Only

    A   Always

    N   Never

    S   Should

3. Ask the client to identify any of their own thought patterns that incorporate the MOANS. Be the child's scribe and write down the thoughts on a piece of paper. For example: "I must get 100% on the test." "I always sit in the front seat." "You never let me go first." Explore the feelings and actions of the client when they are in this rigid thinking space.

4. Become curious with the client about more flexible words that might be used instead of the MOANS:

Instead of:	Try:
Must	Might *or* may
Only	Sometimes
Always	Sometimes
Never	Sometimes
Should	Could

5. Help the client create more flexible versions of their rigid thinking statements. Write these on another piece of paper.

6. On the first copy of the *Rigid/Flexible Thinking Hats* template, write one rigid word on each hat using the MOANS. On the second copy, write one flexible word on each hat. Then cut out each individual hat.

7. Play a game in which all the hats—those with rigid thinking words and those with more flexible thinking words—are mixed up and placed face down in the middle of the table. Put Rigid Rob and Flexible Fred up on a clothesline or magnet board.

8. Have the client choose a hat, read the word, and make up a sentence using this word. For example, if the client picks the hat with the word *always* written on it, they might say, "I always make mistakes."

9. Offer the client either a clothespin or a magnet (depending on whether you're using a clothesline or magnet board), and ask them to secure the hat on either Rigid Rob's head or Flexible Fred's head.

10. It can be fun to bring a caregiver in after the initial teaching and invite them to join the game. Caregivers are often impressed at how much the child has absorbed, and the child can teach the caregiver all about it. Frequently, a deeper understanding of rigid versus flexible thinking is also helpful for the caregiver, both in helping the child and in their own thought life.

RIGID ROB TEMPLATE

FLEXIBLE FRED TEMPLATE

RIGID/FLEXIBLE THINKING HATS TEMPLATE

9.10 A LITTLE BIRDIE TOLD ME*

DESCRIPTION:

This intervention offers a playful, kinesthetically grounded way for clients with troubling cognitive distortions to reduce the impact of these negative thoughts, while identifying and practicing positive replacement thoughts. Many children with a history of trauma carry a set of "should" statements around with them: "I should have been able to keep myself safe. I deserved to be hurt because I disobeyed." These negative thoughts and false attributions can lead to shame and big behaviors if not addressed. This activity helps concretize replacement thoughts for the traumatized client.

TREATMENT GOALS:

- Create physical reminders of thought replacements that the client can carry with them

MATERIALS NEEDED:

- *Little Birdie* template
- Plain paper
- Colorful paper (or felt, fabric, or foam sheets)
- Scissors
- Glue
- Clear tape
- Feathers, googly eyes, or other decorations (optional)

DIRECTIONS:

1. Prior to starting this activity, take note of any cognitive distortions the child or caregiver verbalized during their pre-narrative sessions.

2. At the start of this session, assist the child in writing a list of negative thoughts that they may have encountered following their trauma, suggesting any from your notes that you wish to address. If the child is having difficulty identifying thoughts, you might say something like, "I've been thinking about other times when you've shared parts of your story with me, and I'm remembering some thoughts you shared with me that seem to make you feel worse when you think them over and over again, such as _____."

3. For each cognitive distortion, create an alternate positive self-talk statement. List these in a separate column or on a different piece of paper.

4. Then invite the child to create one or more birds out of the colorful paper. Have them fold the paper in half and then cut out the outline of a bird, creating mirror images. If needed, they can cut out the shapes from the *Little Birdie* template to use as is or to trace onto their own choice of paper. They can also decorate the bird (with feathers,

*Created by Paula Archambault, LMSW, RPT-S.

234

googly eyes, etc.)—just make sure they do so on the outer side of each piece so the two halves can be put back together.

5. Put both pieces together and cover the edges of the bird with clear tape, sealing the edges but leaving a small opening at the bottom edge. Cut off any excess tape.

6. Allow the client to cut or tear the negative thoughts from their list, and encourage them to shred each one into tiny pieces while repeating the positive replacement thought.

7. Then have the client cut or tear the positive thoughts from their list, and invite them to stuff the positive thoughts into the opening on the bird.

8. Explain that the shredded negative thought is the "bird poop" that is discarded as the positive thought helps the bird grow bigger and stronger. Repeat for all the thought distortions on the list.

9. Advise the child if "bird poop" occasionally shows up (i.e., negative cognitions resurface), it is just a reminder of their "little birdie" telling them how strong they're growing. Focus on the bird's song, not the bird's poop!

VARIATION:

Additional birds can be created and made into a mobile to hang in the child's room to reinforce the positive thoughts. This can be especially advantageous if the child has to return to a room where their trauma occurred.

LITTLE BIRDIE TEMPLATE

SPOTLIGHT, SCRIBBLE, AND CHANGE*

DESCRIPTION:

Clients with big behaviors often see problems as catastrophic or overwhelming. Putting a spotlight on a current problem, stressful moment, or event can be the first step toward changing the way the client views the problem and its solutions. The scribbling motions in this intervention (as well as the act of crossing the midline with the body) help provide kinesthetic engagement, thus shifting the paradigm and helping create change.

TREATMENT GOALS:

- Identify a current problem
- Notice cognitive distortions related to the problem
- Engage in bilateral stimulation while transforming the distortion
- Create a paradigm shift related to the problem

MATERIALS NEEDED:

- Loose change
- Flashlight
- Piece of paper and a writing utensil**

DIRECTIONS:

1. Invite the client to write down a problem (a negative belief or troubling issue) around the flashlight on the paper, close to the left edge. Place the loose change close to the right edge of the paper (or you could draw coins or money symbols).

2. Invite the client to quickly scribble back and forth between the flashlight and the "change" on the paper. Allow the client to do this as much as they need until they notice any new thoughts or feelings regarding the identified problem or negative thought. (The bilateral crossing of the page will often stimulate a paradigm shift.)

3. Ask the client if this process has caused any *change* in their perception of the problem. Have them write down this change in thought under the change on the paper.

4. Once the problem has shifted, move the work off the page, further enhancing the shift by having the client move their arms in big, slow circles as they further amplify the changed view of the problem.

5. You can also add deep breath work: Ask the client to notice their body and breath, then scribble again back and forth. Ask them to look at the "change" side and to notice if any new shifts have occurred in the spotlight issue.

---

*Created by Dora Henderson, LMHC, RPT-S, CST.
**Alternatively, sidewalk chalk and crayons make this activity fun because the client can really press and feel more pressure with the body, adding more big-body kinesthetic movement.

9.12 FLEX YOUR MUSCLES

DESCRIPTION:

Clients with big behaviors need help integrating their cognitive responses with their physical responses. Learning how to bring more cognitive control to the body during an escalation requires practice. This intervention pairs intense physical movement (weightlifting) with verbal practice of regulating thoughts. The full-body rehearsal of adaptive thoughts provides useful integrated repetition while helping the client understand that the skill of self-regulation, specifically the skill of accessing helpful cognitions during an escalation, must be strengthened through intentional practice.

TREATMENT GOALS:

- Identify body-based indicators that the client is escalating
- Articulate cognitions that are useful in regulating the body and mind as an escalation is beginning
- Pair kinesthetic experience with cognitive processing

MATERIALS NEEDED:

- Hand weights in 1, 3, 5, and 8 pounds

DIRECTIONS:

1. Explain that when we are stressed, our bodies often take over, bypassing our neocortex and making it difficult to access regulating thoughts. Help the client identify the signs their body gives them when they are feeling stressed and starting to escalate (e.g., clenching their jaw, feeling shaky).

2. Explain that while doing this activity together, you will cause the body to work hard while practicing regulating thoughts.

3. Starting with the lightest set of weights, ask the client to identify a situation that makes them feel stressed. Together, create a positive, regulating statement (e.g., "I can do it!") that they can use to help them get through the situation. Have the client repeat this statement while lifting the weights. You could write down the statement and attach it to the weights to make it more concrete.

4. Explain that just like doing more "reps" in weightlifting makes your muscles stronger so you can lift even heavier weights, doing more reps of positive thoughts makes your mind stronger—calmer and more confident—so you can handle any stressful situation!

5. Provide more challenge to your client (harder situations and heavier weights) as you see appropriate.

MISTAKE SNAKE

DESCRIPTION:

Children with big behaviors sometimes act bad because they feel bad. Negative self-talk (or embedded negative beliefs) is one of the culprits. Children have trouble working with abstract concepts like thoughts and feel more competent when the abstraction is made concrete. This intervention externalizes negative self-talk in the form of a snake who is always hissing at them about their mistakes.

TREATMENT GOALS:

- Externalize negative self-talk
- Learn to boss back the negative self-talk with positive self-talk

MATERIALS NEEDED:

- Snake puppet (any size, color, or shape)
- *Mistake Snake* template
- Shoebox
- Scissors
- Marker

DIRECTIONS:

1. Explain to the client that when we make mistakes, we might beat ourselves up and have really unkind thoughts about ourselves.

2. Ask the client for one unkind thought they think about themselves when they make a mistake.

3. Introduce the snake puppet and explain that you will work together to counter the negative self-talk by having the snake say negative thoughts to the client while the client bosses back the snake to quiet it.

4. Have the client write the negative self-talk statements inside the snake on the *Mistake Snake* template.

5. Explain that you will make a cage for the snake together using the shoebox.

6. Cut strips from the front of the box to make it look like the bars of the cage. Along each bar, write boss back talk or a positive self-talk statement.

7. Be the voice of the Mistake Snake, playfully hissing the negative self-talk at the client. The client gets to say, "Stop! I'm good enough! It doesn't have to be perfect." For each boss back statement the client makes, the snake gets closer and closer to the cage, until it is fully contained.

MISTAKE SNAKE TEMPLATE

9.14 THE WHY CHAIN

DESCRIPTION:

Clients with big behaviors, especially big behaviors that are the result of trauma, can have many false attributions for why the trauma happened. These can impact the client's day-to-day life, resulting in cycles of overresponding or underresponding in a variety of life situations. This intervention invites clients to articulate and then debunk these false attributions. In cases of interpersonal trauma, responsibility is shifted to the perpetrator.

TREATMENT GOALS:

- List all thoughts related to why the hard thing happened
- Explore false attributions and challenge beliefs that lead to false responsibility
- Shift the blame directly onto the perpetrator

MATERIALS NEEDED:

- *Question Mark* template, copied onto several pieces of brightly colored paper
- One piece of plain paper
- Scissors
- Glue
- Markers

DIRECTIONS:

1. With the client, cut out the paper question marks as you verbally process the content in the next steps. The client's approach to the hard discussion will be mitigated by their kinesthetic involvement and visual focus on the paper.

2. Explain that when someone has experienced interpersonal trauma—whether it's physical abuse, sexual abuse, domestic violence, being placed for adoption, parental addictions or mental illness, etc.—they work to make sense of what happened in order to answer the question, "Why did this happen to me?"

3. Write one of the reasons the client thinks the hard thing happened to them inside each question mark, and hang them one from another, much like the monkeys hang from each other in the Barrel of Monkeys® game.

4. One by one, debunk these reasons using psychoeducation, the Socratic method, parent-assisted cognitive interweaves, and so forth. For example, a teenager who believes she was sexually assaulted in her school parking lot because she wore a short skirt may need the clinician to become curious about whether she has worn a short skirt before and if she was assaulted at those times too—the answer being no, the distortion is challenged.

5. As each distortion is challenged, invite the client to cut up each brightly colored question mark, until there is just a pile of colored confetti remaining.

6. On a new sheet of paper, write, in big bubble letters, a statement that places blame back on the perpetrator. Use the confetti as mosaic pieces to fill in the bubble letters.

QUESTION MARK TEMPLATE

FLIPPING THOUGHTS*

DESCRIPTION:

Children with big behaviors often have trouble identifying their thoughts, even when those thoughts lead to actions that are dysregulated or hurtful to themselves or others. Learning about how our thoughts, feelings, and behaviors are all related can be beneficial in helping the child challenge negative thoughts.

TREATMENT GOALS:

- Assist the child and caregiver in understanding how thoughts, feelings, and behaviors are related

- Identify the child's internal negative dialogue to ultimately challenge and correct the maladaptive thoughts

MATERIALS NEEDED:

- *Coder* worksheet
- Construction paper (black, purple, orange, and pink)
- Markers or pens (black, purple, orange, and pink)
- Glue
- Scissors

DIRECTIONS:

1. Talk to the client about the power of our thoughts. You can use the following script:

   "Some kids, and even adults, believe when a thought pops into their brain, it is true. Some kids also believe they cannot control their thoughts and the more they think a particular thought (whether it's negative or positive), the stronger it gets. Even though your brain is super smart, it cannot always recognize the difference between an untrue, unhelpful, negative thought and a true, helpful, positive thought. When we have automatic negative thoughts, our worries increase and it makes our body feel tense, yucky, and uncomfortable. Before we learn about thought problems, we need to learn how to be super coders and code the difference between thoughts, feelings, and behaviors."

2. Give the client the *Coder* worksheet and the purple, orange, and pink markers or pens. Have them color the bubble next to each to code to indicate whether it's a thought, feeling, or behavior.

---

*Created by Tasha Jackson, LCSW, and Lindsey Townsend, LCSW.

3. Introduce the next stage of the activity: "Now that you are a super-duper thought, feeling, and behavior coder, we are going to create a diagram to help you code more!"

4. With the client, take the purple, orange, and pink pieces of construction paper and cut them into approximately three-inch strips. Put these in color-coordinated piles.

5. Together, write down as many thoughts as the client can generate on the purple strips.* Write feelings on the orange strips and behaviors on the pink strips. Keep one piece of each color and write *thought*, *feeling*, or *behavior* on the appropriate color.

6. On the black construction paper, create a triangle with the three labels. Have the client glue the "thought" slip at the top of the triangle, the "feeling" slip on the bottom right, and the "behavior" slip on the bottom left. This forms a reusable board that you can use to work with the client on their thoughts, feelings, and behaviors.

7. Returning to the thought cards, write the opposite of each negative thought on the back of the card (negative → positive). Place all the thought cards in a stack, negative side up.

8. Take turns with the client choosing a thought card. Put the thought on the board and go through the feeling and behavior the child would experience in response to that thought. Then flip the thought card over and show the POWER of our thoughts!

---

*Sometimes children have a difficult time coming up with thoughts. Tell the client you will work hard on some thoughts, and be sure to choose some you believe the client may be experiencing. When working with a specific trauma, be sure to add common maladaptive thoughts that children experience to the pile of thoughts. This will ensure you are able to open the conversation and discuss potentially shameful thoughts the child may not want to bring up. For example, a child who has been sexually abused may not understand their body has an automated response and that feeling pleasure is common and out of the child's control. Adding the negative thought "There is something wrong with me because it felt good when the abuser touched my body" can open the dialogue for you to discuss how bodies automatically respond to touches and how many children and adults have the same thought. Then assist the child in correcting the thought to "My body automatically responds to touch, and I had no control over how my body reacted. I am okay and there is nothing wrong with me."

CODER WORKSHEET

This worksheet will help you learn how to code thoughts, feelings, and behaviors. **Thoughts** are the things we say to ourselves inside our heads. **Feelings** are the emotions we have inside our bodies. **Behaviors** are what we do with our bodies or how our body reacts.

Let's look at the list below and start coding:

Thoughts with purple   **Feelings with orange**   **Behaviors with pink**

- Worried
- Sad
- Chill
- Safe
- Ashamed
- Lonely
- Courageous
- Running
- Walking
- Crying
- Smiling
- She hates me
- I did great on that test
- Scared
- Safe
- I look pretty
- I'll be okay
- My life stinks
- Punching a wall
- Worried
- I will never be okay
- Excited
- Taking a test
- He doesn't like me
- I should have said no
- Eating pizza
- Lonely
- Singing a song

- Taking deep breaths
- Ashamed
- Brave
- My hair is ugly
- This is the worst day
- My family is disappointed in me
- I don't have any friends
- Kicking my friend
- Slamming my bedroom door
- I will never be as good as other kids
- I am not good enough
- I am a bad kid
- I am not lovable
- Angry
- Bored
- Guilty
- Hurt
- No one understands me
- Standing tall
- Embarrassed
- Falling in the hallway
- Face turns red
- Jumping over a fence
- Stomachache
- Vomiting
- Biting my fingernails
- Fearless

ten

Storykeeping: Holding Hard Stories and Building Coherent Narratives

----

Children with big behaviors have often experienced hard things that leave them with disjointed images, intrusive sense memories, sudden attachment ruptures, and overwhelming feelings of terror or helplessness. After these scary experiences, a vacuum of silence often remains. Caregivers are unavailable or so steeped in their own shame or other big emotions that they do not provide structured stories to their children. These children need interventions that help bring the hard story in the room and that build a coherent narrative. In the TraumaPlay model, therapists do so by assuming the role of Storykeeper, in which they look at the current big behavior and trace it back to its earliest origins and then help the client make sense of how the two are connected.

For example, consider the case of Billy, a four-year-old boy who was adopted domestically at birth. Billy was born addicted to methamphetamines. The nurses and doctors who took care of him in those early days reported that Billy experienced the worst case of withdrawal they had ever seen. He was on the highest doses of morphine allowed and continued to seize, cry inconsolably, shake, pass out, and vomit. Billy's adoptive mother, who was there from birth, spoke of holding him and rocking him but being unable to soothe him. Now, at four years old, this little one is avoidant and unable to ask for what he needs. Instead, he makes demands and begins to tantrum when his parents try to take care of his hurts. Billy is in need of a story.

The continuing growth for therapists who work as Storykeepers is to figure out how much truth to tell and how to share that truth in a way that brings context and understanding to the big behaviors in developmentally sensitive terms. Deciding if, when, and to what extent caregivers are involved in the actual building of narratives depends on each individual case conceptualization, but generally speaking, caregivers who already embody the roles of Safe Boss and Nurturer may be very useful in the storytelling process.

However, in systems where intergenerational trauma is at play, or in systems where caregivers may have intense emotional responses to holding hard pieces of the child's story, caregivers may need support from the therapist in collateral sessions prior to being in the room with the child for trauma narrative work. In these instances, the therapist can deliver parts of the trauma narrative to the caregiver so the therapist can hold the brunt of the caregiver's big emotion, stretch the caregiver's containment ability, and role-play the response that the caregiver will have in the dyadic session with the child.

Sometimes children have the factual account of a story—the logical, linear, linguistic narrative—but the story doesn't integrate the affectual components (feelings), the cognitive components (thoughts), or the somatic components (body-based experiences) of the scary thing that happened. When trauma has happened pre-linguistically, children may have the body-based experiences stored as implicit memories with no conscious sense of remembering, and they may need help identifying the source of these bodily reactions. When a child is experiencing the intrusive or avoidance symptoms of PTSD, building a coherent narrative becomes even more important. This chapter offers a host of interventions that help to playfully structure storytelling when it is needed.

10.1 PUZZLES WITH CAREGIVERS

DESCRIPTION:

Children who have experienced complex trauma may need help making sense of these events. Visual images, feelings, and sensory experiences can be encoded in memories that are separate from the linear, linguistic story of what happened. They may have big behaviors that result from the implicit memory system, perhaps because the trauma occurred pre-linguistically. In these cases, it may be helpful to have the caregiver offer details of the story. This intervention encourages caregivers and children to work together to fill in the gaps in family stories.

TREATMENT GOALS:

- Enlist the caregiver as a helper in building a coherent narrative
- Explore the timeline of family events and create snapshots of key moments
- Fill in the gaps, when possible, in the client's trauma narrative

MATERIALS NEEDED:

- Several make-your-own puzzles (blank puzzles)
- Pictures provided by the family, sized to fit the puzzle template

- Glue
- Craft knife
- Crayons or markers

DIRECTIONS:

1. In advance, ask the caregiver to gather photos taken during key family moments. These should include both positive moments (e.g., developmental milestones, special achievements, family vacations) and a few photos associated with difficult things that have happened (e.g., illness, accidents, natural disasters, loss of loved ones). Let the family know to keep a copy of each photo, as they will be cut up into puzzle pieces. If the child was not in the caregiver's care in the beginning, they can draw pictures of what they know or imagine from the time before they were together.

2. Beginning with a safe, sweet, connected time (whenever possible), glue the picture onto the top of the puzzle. Then cut along the already defined puzzle pieces from the back side, and jumble up the pieces.

3. Talk about what each person remembers about the time depicted in the puzzle. Explain that having multiple perspectives on the same event can help us fill in the gaps, providing each other's missing pieces of the puzzle.*

---

*In some cases, the client or dyad may decide they want each puzzle piece to represent one thing that happened during the traumatic event and to spontaneously sequence the events themselves. Other times, children need more titration or exposure to the hard things and will ask to have some puzzle pieces depict happy events from their lives and some represent harder things. Follow the client's lead.

4. Use this same process with a picture from the hard thing that happened. If there are no pictures, have the caregiver and child decide together what image they want to draw on the puzzle. Again, break up the puzzle pieces and have them work together to put it back together while becoming curious about thoughts, feelings, and sensory impressions experienced by both or either person during the trauma.

5. If multiple puzzles are completed over multiple sessions, you could create a book of puzzles for the family to take with them from therapy.

EXCAVATING HARD THINGS

DESCRIPTION:

Big behaviors in children can be the body's manifestation of trauma. Although children benefit from activating their thinking brain and having their left hemisphere engaged while naming the hard things that have happened, they may be hard-pressed to do so unless they are kinesthetically grounded in play. Burying the hard things in modeling clay and then excavating them pairs verbalization of potential trauma targets with tactile involvement.

TREATMENT GOALS:

- Identify stressors, traumas, or anxieties that need to be processed
- Identify adaptive coping strategies that protect the client from the full effects of stressful events

MATERIALS NEEDED:

- Modeling clay
- Small, hard objects such as LEGO® bricks, dried beans, grains of rice, or dried pasta
- Tweezers (otherwise your fingers will do the job)

DIRECTIONS:

1. Explain to the child that you are going to become archaeologists together, burying small objects in the modeling clay and then uncovering them.

2. Offer the child the modeling clay to kinesthetically explore. The client can warm it in their hands, flatten it out, and so on.

3. Then invite the child to push a variety of small, hard objects into the modeling clay, making sure each piece is fully embedded. Cooperatively decide what objects to use for this activity. Small LEGO pieces are especially engaging.

4. Once the hard objects are embedded in the clay, invite the client to hunt for the objects using the tweezers. Once they find a piece, they will extract it with the tweezers while they verbalize one stressor, trauma, or hard thing that has happened. This can be a fun, titrated way to gather an initial list of targets for trauma narrative work or EMDR work. It also mitigates the approach to the more difficult content with play and kinesthetic involvement.

5. If using hard objects with defined edges (like LEGO pieces), you can also mention how the modeling clay offers some protection against the sharp edges of the hard things that have happened, and name adaptive coping strategies that can help the child harness resiliencies as they move forward in treatment.

VARIATIONS:

When a caregiver is included, each person makes their own creation, and a shared narrative can be enhanced as they listen to each other talk through their excavations. In a telehealth session, the client (and their caregiver, if participating) can get creative in finding materials within their environment that will work for this activity. Some dyads make ice cream sundaes and choose various mixers to be the hard things: chocolate chips, granola, and so on. Others use shaving cream and pennies; still others make mud pies in the backyard and put rocks or sticks inside for excavation. Chopsticks can also be used as an excavation tool for more novelty.

10.3 THE TODDLER BOOK

DESCRIPTION:

Young children with big behaviors often escalate when they don't have the words to express themselves. When hard things happen in the lives of toddlers in particular, it helps their development and understanding dramatically if their caregivers can narrate the events for them. This narration brings coherence and can siphon off some of the stress of the event. This intervention helps caregivers deliver coherent narratives to their toddlers while providing nurturing touch and a playful experience.

TREATMENT GOALS:

- Provide caregiver-assisted cognitive interweaves for children who may only understand parts of what happened during a stressful event
- Amplify a coherent narrative for the child as the caregiver tells the story
- Encourage the child to add on to the story

MATERIALS NEEDED:

- None

DIRECTIONS:

1. Explain that sometimes young children only absorb certain aspects of a stressful event and may benefit from narration from their caregiver.
2. Invite the caregiver to sit with their legs out in front of them.
3. Place the toddler on the caregiver's legs, facing them.
4. Have the caregiver hold both of the toddler's hands, bringing their arms together across their body to the toddler's right side (the caregiver's left side).
5. Have the caregiver pretend the toddler's arms are the cover of a book and read the title out loud (for example, *The Time the Car Made a Great Big Noise*). Encourage the caregiver to look at the toddler's arms (the toddler is normally watching the caregiver's face carefully).*
6. The caregiver then opens the toddler's arms wide. They verbalize the first sentence of the story while "reading" it on the toddler's right arm, then say the second sentence of the story while "reading" it on their left arm. Then the caregiver should put the toddler's arms together as if they are turning the page and start again, repeating until they reach the end of the story.
7. If the toddler interrupts with a detail of their own, this should be incorporated right away. If the toddler does not offer any input, you or the caregiver can ask gently, "What happened next?" in case they have a detail to add.

---

*When you remove the expectation of direct eye contact, it lowers the child's defenses and can allow the toddler to listen to the story without feeling any pressure to respond to the story.

10.4 SECRET BOOK SAFE*

DESCRIPTION:

Clients who exhibit big behaviors following trauma can feel a lot of pressure to keep secrets. This intervention turns the tables on secrecy, offering a safe, contained space for the client to start sharing with the therapist. Even if the client is not ready to talk to the therapist directly about trauma content, the book safe offers a boundaried space in which the client can put secrets, thoughts, feelings, and so on. Sometimes these are written and sometimes they are drawn. The creation of the book safe itself can take several sessions to complete.

TREATMENT GOALS:

- Reinforce personal boundaries
- Keep thoughts safe until the client feels prepared to disclose them
- Provide safety from scary thoughts and feelings
- Contain intrusive thoughts until they can be processed and discarded

MATERIALS NEEDED:

- An assortment of hardcover books (that can be repurposed)
- Glue or another adhesive, such as Mod Podge®
- Paintbrushes
- Plastic/polycarbonate sheets or transparency film
- Razor knife and blades
- Ruler or straight edge

DIRECTIONS:

1. Invite the client to select a book. They may want to choose one that won't stand out or look out of place in their room or among their schoolbooks.**

2. Assist the client in sectioning the book into three parts: approximately ten to twenty pages for the top and bottom sections, and the remaining pages in the middle section (which will have the center of each page cut out for the "safe"). Place a plastic sheet between each section.

---

*Created by Paula Archambault, LMSW, RPT-S.

**A discarded textbook can be used in this way and carried in a child's backpack to provide a secure place to hold scary or intrusive thoughts and feelings that may arise during their school day. They can write or draw them on a small piece of paper and crumple them up to put inside the safe until you and the client can work together to get rid of them.

3. Assist the client in applying glue with a paintbrush to saturate the three edges of the top and bottom sections. The pages should not be glued to each other. Use this time to discuss the types of thoughts, feelings, or small items the client may wish to keep in their book safe. Close the book tightly. Paint the edges of the middle section with glue. Let the glue dry.

4. Open the book and remove the plastic. Use a straight edge to define the area to be removed from the center pages, leaving at least a one-inch border on the outside edges of the book. Use a razor knife to carefully cut out the center of the pages in the middle section.* Glue the middle section to the bottom section. Apply several layers of glue to the three outside edges of the book. Let the glue dry.

5. Invite the client to decorate the cover if they would like.

6. Discuss with the client which parts of their story (thoughts, feelings, or details of the trauma story itself) will go in the book safe and where the safe will be kept. This offer of containment invites a holding space for aspects of the trauma to be held and can be a bridge to more open sharing later in treatment.

*The use of a sharp knife can be a powerful intervention with teenage clients struggling with self-harm thoughts or behaviors. Allowing them to hold and use the knife in a constructive way as they discuss their thoughts of cutting and self-harm can provide tremendous healing and insight for both you and them.

10.5 TIMELINE GARDEN*

DESCRIPTION:

Clients with big behaviors, especially those who have experienced multiple traumas, may have unintegrated pieces of trauma, stored like shrapnel in the brain. Creating a timeline is a tried-and-true way to begin sequencing traumatic events for clients. In the TraumaPlay model, glimpses or snapshots may need to be gathered in the early days of treatment before a client will be ready to do timeline work. Once they are, the timeline garden (Goodyear-Brown & Hyatt, 2020) offers a gentle, playful way for the client to identify both delightful and difficult moments of their early life.

TREATMENT GOALS:

- Increase coherence of the client's life story
- Articulate meaningful moments from the client's history, giving equal acknowledgment to the importance of both the joyful moments and the harder moments
- Create a trauma narrative with the client

MATERIALS NEEDED:

- Long piece of paper (such as butcher paper)
- Markers
- Green duct tape

DIRECTIONS:

1. Explain to the client that you will be creating a timeline garden to document the key events in their life to date.
2. Place a line of green duct tape horizontally through the middle of the paper to represent the ground.
3. Explain that major events that were delightful, joyful, or happy go above the grass line and will be represented with flowers.
4. Explain that major events that were hard, yucky, or heavy will be depicted with stones or mud puddles below the grass line.
5. Ask the client to draw their major life events on the timeline. You can return to this activity in the future to continue adding events.

VARIATION:

If preferred, or to harness the benefits of doing therapeutic work in nature, move outside and find actual flowers and stones to represent the life events.

---

*Created by Eleah Hyatt, MA, LMFT, RPT.

DESCRIPTION:

Children who have experienced chronic trauma have unprocessed narratives inside of them. These untold stories often come out in their big behaviors. Bringing more coherence to the stories of what happened can help clients come into deeper levels of regulation. This intervention offers one way to enhance the trauma narrative.

TREATMENT GOALS:

- Invite a telling of the trauma narrative

MATERIALS NEEDED:

- Two shoeboxes of the same size
- Art supplies (colored paper, glitter, glue, yarn, toothpicks, popsicle sticks, etc.)**

DIRECTIONS:

1. Offer the client the first shoebox and invite them to decorate the house as they believe other people saw their home from the outside (by decorating the outside of the box).

2. When they've finished, ask them to show what it was truly like inside the house (by decorating the inside of the shoebox).

3. Offer your client privacy while working on their box if this makes them more comfortable. You could sit away from them, use a cardboard partition, or provide aluminum foil that they can use to cover their work.

4. When the client is ready, hold space for them to explain their house (trauma narrative) through the project. Allow them to show their shoebox, or to open and close the aluminum foil, as they feel ready. Allow some time in between the narration of the first box and the work with the second box.

5. The process for the second box is almost identical, only this time, ask the client to decorate their current house (or their future/dream house) from the outside as people see it and from the inside as they would like it to be. As before, allow the client to show the box and narrate the contents as they are ready.

6. Detail for them how much they have learned and grown to be able to express their needs, rights, and desires through the second house.

7. The two houses can serve as a reference for future sessions to show the client their strength, endurance, bravery, and courage.

---

*Created by Jennifer Tapley, MEd, and Michelle Codington, MS, LMFT, RPT-S, CFPT.

**The client may make specific requests if there are additional items they need in order to make a more accurate representation of either shoebox.

SAND IN MY EYES

DESCRIPTION:

Children who have experienced trauma may have unprocessed sense memories (tastes, smells, sounds, tactile sensations, visual images) connected to the trauma. Children are often unwilling to burden their caregiver with the details of the trauma for fear of overwhelming them. These unprocessed sense memories then tend to come out in big behaviors. This intervention offers a structured invitation for children to share visual images absorbed during the trauma.

TREATMENT GOALS:

- Identify details of the traumatic event that were visually encoded
- Sequence the visual images and integrate them with other narrative elements
- Mitigate potentially overwhelming content by engaging the child in kinesthetic activity

MATERIALS NEEDED:

- Googly eyes of various sizes
- Sand tray
- Glue
- *What I Saw* recording sheet (or other paper)

DIRECTIONS:

1. Ask the client if they've ever had sand in their eyes. If they have, invite them to share their experience. Having sand in our eyes is uncomfortable, even painful, until we can get the sand out. It may even hurt more for a matter of seconds or minutes in the process of removing the irritant.

2. Explain that sense memories related to traumatic events can feel the same way. Normalize the idea that children and teens may have seen things during a trauma that they have not felt comfortable sharing with their caregivers. Many children have encoded intense visual images but attempt to keep these images to themselves, as they don't want to compromise a caregiver's ability to care for them by overwhelming them with graphic visual imagery.

3. Show the sand tray and the various sizes of googly eyes to the client.

4. Explain that different visual images carry different power for us. Sprinkle some small, medium, and large googly eyes in the sand tray and cover them up.

5. Invite the client to hide-and-seek the googly eyes with their fingers. When they find one, have them share one visual image related to the trauma. If it is a small googly eye, they might share something that doesn't hold much power for them. A medium googly eye could represent a picture in their head that bothers them sometimes. A large one might represent an intrusive visual image encoded during the traumatic event.

6. Write down the descriptions the client shares. You can glue the googly eyes in sequential order on a piece of paper or use the *What I Saw* recording sheet.

WHAT I SAW RECORDING SHEET

What I saw during the scary thing that happened:

👁	
👁	
👁	
👁	
👁	
👁	
👁	
👁	
👁	

10.8 GOOGLY-EYE HOP

DESCRIPTION:

Children who have experienced trauma may have unprocessed sense memories, including a series of visual images, related to the trauma. When left unintegrated, these images may trigger big behaviors, including aggression, impulsivity, and sleep problems. One path toward integration is to ground children in the strength of their bodies by having them jump from eye to eye while verbally sharing their visual memories.

TREATMENT GOALS:

- Identify details of the traumatic event that were visually encoded

- Sequence the visual images and integrate them with other narrative elements

- Mitigate potentially overwhelming content by engaging the child in kinesthetic activity

MATERIALS NEEDED:

- Giant googly eyes (or large printed images of eyes)

- Small googly eyes

- Paper and markers

- Glue

DIRECTIONS:

1. Invite the client to explore the variety of sizes of googly eyes available and introduce the giant googly eyes.

2. Lay out at least four extra-large googly eyes at least one foot apart, like stepping-stones, on the floor.

3. Ask the client to stand on the first googly eye and to name one visual detail encoded during the trauma—"one thing you saw during the scary thing that happened." If you have done previous narrative work, the client may benefit from the question being framed chronologically: "What did you see first?" "What did you see next?"

4. Invite the client to jump from one googly eye to another while sequencing the visual input.

5. As the game is played, you can glue small googly eyes down the left side of a piece of paper and write down the child's explanations of what they saw. You can also use the *What I Saw* recording sheet (from activity 10.7).

VARIATION:

If a high challenge level may increase the client's enjoyment of the activity, you can encourage them to pretend that "toxic pig snot" is under the stepping-stones (and if you fall off the googly eye island, you get it on you—yuck!).

10.9 WALK IT THROUGH

DESCRIPTION:

Unmetabolized trauma memories, especially those related to sensory details of the trauma, can be stored as implicit memories that are easily activated in bodily responses, sometimes leading to big behaviors in children. This playful intervention provides a novel way to name smells and sounds associated with the trauma, which lessens the impact of working with such hard content (Goodyear-Brown, 2019).

TREATMENT GOALS:

- Identify sensory memories related to traumatic events
- Explore auditory and olfactory trauma reminders
- Invite sequencing of sensory experiences to build a more coherent narrative, integrating sensory memories into the story of what happened

MATERIALS NEEDED:

- Wind-up plastic novelty nose toy
- Wind-up plastic novelty ear toy
- Colored ribbon
- Sticky notes
- Writing utensil

DIRECTIONS:

1. Explain that when scary things happen, our bodies encode the sights, smells, sounds, tastes, and tactile sensations associated with the scary or stressful event.

2. Roll out a length of ribbon along the table while explaining that you are going to explore the smells and sounds connected to the traumatic event.

3. Introduce the wind-up ear and set it on the far-left end of the ribbon. Ask the client to share the basic chronology of the traumatic event (or you may already have this information). Write down each part of the sequence on a sticky note and place these under the ribbon to form a timeline. For example, the child's narrative sequence of events may be: "The smoke detector went off, I woke up, I called for my mom, I ran out of the room and down the stairs, and eventually the fire truck came."

4. Wind up the ear toy and set it down so it starts walking along the ribbon timeline. As it reaches each part of the story, ask the client to share the sounds they associate with that moment. Write these sounds down on sticky notes and add them to the timeline.

5. Repeat this process for the wind-up nose, adding the smells associated with each part of the story to the timeline.

FULL-CIRCLE SAND TRAYS

DESCRIPTION:

This intervention is meant to help build coherence in shared family narratives about hard things. When more than one member of a family has experienced a traumatic event, such as the death of loved one, a car accident, or a house fire, it can be healing for the group to create a sand tray together that expresses each person's journey through the traumatic event in a circular way.

TREATMENT GOALS:

- Build coherent narratives of shared stressful events

MATERIALS NEEDED:

- Circular sand tray
- Sand tray miniatures

DIRECTIONS:

1. Ask the family to identify a traumatic event that they experienced together.

2. Explain that they will depict their journey through the trauma, starting at the top of the sand tray and working their way around the tray clockwise, tracking specific events, thoughts, or sensory impressions along the way.

3. Have each person reflect on how the trauma began. For example, if the identified trauma was the death of a grandmother due to cancer, family members might remember the family dinner where the grandmother first told them she was sick. Each family member is invited to choose a miniature that represents their experience of learning about her cancer.

4. Each family member continues to choose miniatures to represent the stages of their journey through the stressful event.

5. Afterward, help each individual participant share their full-circle experience of the trauma.

6. Last, provide time to process what each family member learned about the experiences of the others as they made the Full-Circle Sand Tray together.

Graduation: Making a Meaningful Goodbye

Change is hard work. It can also be fun, playful, and connected, but risk is involved every time we attempt to shift a paradigm, stretch our windows of tolerance, connect more deeply with each other, or use our voices to ask for what we need. It's hard work to trust that if we identify and share the vulnerable feelings underneath our anger, we will learn to avoid becoming destructive in our anger. It's hard work to trust that if we do things differently in our relationships, we will experience those relationships differently. Change happens over time, and clients may not even realize how much they have changed until we start remarking on their treatment gains and begin talking about termination.

In TraumaPlay, we prefer the word *graduation* to termination. We believe in the power of making a meaningful goodbye. Many children with big behaviors have experienced multiple ACEs (Anda et al., 2006), which, by their nature, create abrupt attachment ruptures. A parent hits a crisis point in active addiction and abruptly leaves to rehab for two months. In more cases than I would expect, children are told very little about the abrupt departure and aren't given a chance to make a meaningful goodbye. Or a parent who was incarcerated suddenly returns to the home, with no discussion of where they've been, what they learned, how they grew, or what they missed. The higher the number of ACEs a child has experienced, the greater the number of goodbyes they have had to endure from which no meaning was made. For these clients, it is doubly important that we honor the relationship and their therapeutic work with an intentional closure process.

When working with children, therapists can experience a different kind of countertransference than they do when working with adult clients. With adult clients, it is easier to separate our sense of personal responsibility for therapeutic change from the adults' choices to do the work or not. The responsibility therapists can feel for their minor clients—and the reality that these little ones need Nurturers, Safe Bosses, and Storykeepers, and may have limited abilities to choose for themselves—can muddy the waters when it is time to say goodbye. Therapists can back away from the feelings of loss, sadness, guilt, anger, or confusion that can arise within the client, the therapist, or both. The activities in this chapter help clinicians lean into the goodbye process instead.

TraumaPlay clinicians begin the process of saying goodbye at least four sessions before the final session. In almost all cases, they work with the client to create a memento (e.g., an artistic creation, a craft, a container of some sort) that serves as a transitional object to mark the set of relational experiences, therapeutic change, and skill development absorbed in the course of treatment. During these four sessions, clinicians reflect on the client's growth, review coping strategies the client can continue to use during stressful times, discuss meaningful shared moments in the therapeutic process, and consider hopes and dreams for the future. The interventions that follow are all useful during this graduation process.

GRADUATION CAPS

DESCRIPTION:

When clients graduate from treatment, it is important to mark the hard work they have done. Making individualized graduation caps, complete with tassels, is one way to help clients reflect on their growth in treatment; rehearse any new skills, knowledge, or narrative integrations that they will take with them; and celebrate their accomplishment.

TREATMENT GOALS:

- Reflect on the client's therapeutic growth
- Celebrate the client's hard work in therapy
- Mark the achievement of treatment goals while making a meaningful goodbye

MATERIALS NEEDED:

- 8.5" × 11" sheets of card stock
- Colorful yarn or string
- Markers
- Stapler and/or tape
- Scissors

DIRECTIONS:

1. Explain that as part of graduating from treatment, the client will create a graduation cap. (Prefabricated cardboard hats can be used, but most children and teens prefer to make their own.)

2. Starting with a piece of card stock, cut an eight-inch square. The remaining strip of paper will be three inches wide and can serve as the bottom of the graduation cap. (For larger heads, cut additional strips of paper and tape or staple them together.)

3. Invite the client to reflect on their therapeutic goals and to write down their clinical milestones, favorite activities, and therapeutic accomplishments on the top of the graduation cap.

4. On the band underneath the graduation cap, you (or the client's caregiver) can write positive affirmations. For example: "You have worked hard!" "You have learned a lot!" "You learned to control your anger!" "You know what your body needs!"

5. To create the tassel, cut several pieces of yarn and have client make a positive self-statement ("I am...") to represent each strand of the tassel.

6. Use tape or a stapler to put all the pieces of the graduation cap together.

TREATMENT TAKEAWAYS

DESCRIPTION:

Clients with big behaviors often learn a series of very practical skills during treatment, including how to self-regulate, how to use their voices and bodies more effectively, how to focus on positive cognitions, and how to repair relationship ruptures. During the termination phase, this intervention offers a playful way to reflect on the learning and growth that clients will take with them after treatment ends.

TREATMENT GOALS:

- Review the treatment goals the client has achieved

- Concretize therapeutic learning by writing it down

- Create a transitional object for the client to take home from treatment

MATERIALS NEEDED:

- Chinese food takeout boxes (can be found in white or in other colors and patterns)

- Coloring utensils

- Slips of paper

- Ingredients and equipment to make fortune cookies*

DIRECTIONS:

1. As clients prepare to end therapy, they have normally achieved mastery of certain skills, strategies, behavior patterns, or ways of relating to others based on the goals established early in treatment. Invite the client to reflect on these.

2. Write down treatment takeaways on small slips of paper. This intervention can be especially meaningful if you also invite the client's caregivers and other family members to contribute affirmations of the client's growth.

3. Make fortune cookies together, placing the paper slips inside the cookies.**

4. Invite the client to decorate the outside of their takeout box by drawing pictures and/or writing phrases that represent their progress. These may include activities completed within the therapy room, restructured cognitions, new skills, mantras, support people, and so forth.

5. Put the completed fortune cookies in the box for the client to take home.

---

*You can find recipes for hand-shaped fortune cookies online, or you can streamline the process by using a fortune cookie maker and premade mix. Check with the caregiver in advance for food allergies.
**If your clinical environment does not support actually making cookies in session, alternatives include making origami fortune cookies (where the "cookie" is also made of paper) or attaching the treatment takeaways to premade cookies using dollops of frosting, decorative ribbons, etc.

11.3 MENDING BROKEN PIECES OF MY HEART*

DESCRIPTION:

For many children and caregivers who have experienced relational trauma and attachment injuries within their relationship, it can feel as if their heart has been torn into pieces. Although the repair process is healing, it can be painful at first. However, as trust is rebuilt or created for the first time, the nature of their relationship can become stronger, healthier, and *secure enough* (Byng-Hall, 1995). In this expressive arts intervention, the Japanese art of kintsugi is adapted to represent the healing of the relationship as represented by the heart. Kintsugi is the Japanese art of repairing broken pottery using gold or platinum dust within the lacquer to mend the areas of breakage and restore the pottery to its original shape. In this adaptation, clients can use golden thread, puffy paint, or masking tape to represent the healing their hearts have experienced.

TREATMENT GOALS:

- Increase felt safety and security within the caregiver-child relationship
- Acknowledge and address relationship repair within the caregiver-child relationship
- Increase the child's sense of self-worth and self-esteem

MATERIALS NEEDED:

- Blank paper
- Watercolors or markers
- Scissors
- Gold puffy paint, a brush, and masking tape (or gold thread and a needle)

DIRECTIONS:

1. Invite the caregiver and child to each draw a large heart on a piece of blank paper. They can choose to cut out the heart shape if desired. Then allow them to decorate or color the heart as they desire.

2. Direct the caregiver-child dyad to make rips or tears in the heart to represent their trauma experiences or attachment injuries. You may want to explore or process the rips or tears, or this can be done in silence, depending upon their therapeutic needs.

3. To represent their healing process, invite the caregiver and child to begin repairing the rips or tears. They can use the gold puffy paint (along with the masking tape, if needed) to reconnect the edges, or they can use gold thread and a needle to stitch the edges back together. Invite them to share their thoughts and feelings as they repair their heart together.

---

*Created by Clair Mellenthin, LCSW, RPT-S.

COOKIE JAR*

DESCRIPTION:

Making a meaningful goodbye is important when ending treatment with our clients. This intervention offers a playful, nurturing way to help clients count down to their final session while rehearsing coping strategies they have learned over the course of treatment.

TREATMENT GOALS:

- Verbalize an understanding of when and how therapy will end
- Provide a positive termination experience

MATERIALS NEEDED:

- Jar or container
- Adhesive label
- Marker
- Five cookies**
- *Cookie Jar* handout
- *Cookies* template
- Scissors

DIRECTIONS:

1. Introduce this intervention to the client when there are five sessions left.
2. Write the client's name on the adhesive label and stick it on the outside of the jar (e.g., "Lisa's Cookie Jar").
3. Place five cookies in the jar.
4. Give the *Cookie Jar* handout to the client and follow the directions together for the next four sessions.
5. During the last session, print the *Cookies* template. Cut out the paper cookies and write a coping statement on each. For example:
   - I learned ways to help myself feel better.
   - All my feelings are okay.
   - There are always safe adults to talk to.
   - I can feel good about my proud moments.
   - I can give myself a hug to feel better.

---

*Reprinted with permission from *Creative CBT Interventions for Children with Anxiety* (Lowenstein, 2016).
**Check with the caregiver in advance for food allergies.

6. You can also include the following instructions for "cookie breathing" on one of the paper cookies. This provides the child with a visual prompt to use deep breathing during times of stress:

"Imagine you just baked your favorite cookies and they're coming hot out of the oven. Smell the yummy cookies by slowly breathing in through your nose for four seconds. Cool down the yummy cookies by slowly breathing out through your mouth for four seconds."

7. Fold the paper cookies and put them in the cookie jar for the client to take home with them. This provides the child with a positive ending experience and a transitional object to take home at the end of therapy.

COOKIE JAR HANDOUT

You have worked hard in therapy and you have learned so much! This means you are almost ready to stop coming to therapy. This activity is called the Cookie Jar. It will help you understand when and how therapy will end so you will feel ready.

Open the cookie jar, take out one cookie (only one!), and eat the cookie. The remaining cookies in the jar show how many more times you will be coming here. There are four cookies left in the jar. So you will be coming here four more times, and then you and I will be saying goodbye to each other. Place the lid on the cookie jar.

Ask me to say something you have learned in therapy and to tell you why you are almost ready to stop coming to therapy.

We'll repeat this activity at the end of our next three sessions (eat one cookie from the cookie jar, count the remaining cookies in the jar, and say how many more times you will be coming to therapy). At the end of the three sessions, there will be one cookie left in the cookie jar, which means you will come to therapy one last time. The last time you come will be special. It will be a celebration of all the hard work you have done in therapy. It will be a time for us to say a last goodbye to each other.

At the end of your last session, you will get to eat the last cookie left in the jar.

COOKIES TEMPLATE

FAMILY FLOWERPOT

DESCRIPTION:

This exercise encourages each member of the family to reflect on the nuggets of knowledge, insight, relational connection, or specific skill development that occurred over the course of treatment. Each family member must make a shift in order for the family system to move toward optimal health. This activity also reminds family members that they must nurture the growth made in therapy in order for continued growth to occur.

TREATMENT GOALS:

- Reflect on the treatment gains of individual family members
- Verbalize growth in the family system as a unit
- Create a transitional object for the client to take home from treatment
- Provide a future template for nurturing continued growth

MATERIALS NEEDED:

- Tiny flowerpots (one for each family member)
- Large flowerpot
- Paint
- Paintbrushes
- Packets of flower seeds
- Soil

DIRECTIONS:

1. As family members prepare to end therapy, they have normally mastered certain skills, strategies, behavior patterns, or ways of relating to others based on the goals established early in treatment. Invite each family member to reflect on these.

2. Give a flowerpot to each family member and encourage them to explore the seed packs.

3. Invite each person to paint words and symbols on their flowerpot that represent their individual growth.

4. Have each person fill their pot with soil and ask them to choose a seed they would like to plant. As they plant their seeds, invite each person to talk about their growth.

5. When each family member is done with their individual pot, present a larger flowerpot to the family as a whole.

6. Invite the family to reflect on the changes they have seen in the overall health or patterns of behavior in the family.

7. Then instruct the family to decorate the family flowerpot in a cooperative process— also adding soil and seeds to the pot—until the family flowerpot is complete.

8. Discuss with the family that they can take this object home, and with consistent care and watering, they will be able to visualize their continued growth.

MEMORY MARKERS

DESCRIPTION:

Many clients benefit from the use of transitional objects in the goodbye process. Children with big behaviors may especially enjoy having some sort of concrete reminder of the therapeutic relationship. This activity offers one way to provide these markers during the final session.

TREATMENT GOALS:

- Review the treatment goals the client has achieved
- Rehearse shared memories of the time spent together in the therapy room
- Give the client something concrete to use as a reminder of the therapeutic relationship

MATERIALS NEEDED:

- A special container to serve as a treasure chest
- A variety of stones and pebbles
- A paint pen or permanent marker

DIRECTIONS:

1. Invite the client to share their memories from therapy with you. The following prompts can be used:

   a. What was one big feeling you had during our first session?

   b. What was your favorite art activity?

   c. What was your favorite game to play together?

   d. Can you remember a time when you got really frustrated? Sad? Scared?

2. If the client has trouble remembering specific moments, you can offer memories of your own.

3. Explain that when your clients graduate from therapy, they get to pick a special stone from the treasure chest to take with them. Offer them the treasure chest, and invite them to pick one stone that they'd like to keep.

4. Once they have chosen a stone, ask them to place it in your palm. Put one hand under the stone and one hand over it, cupping it in your hands.

5. Explain that you are going to squeeze your hands together very hard and press all of your warm memories about the client into the stone. You can also have the child hold the stone in their hands, with you pressing your hands around the child's hands, offering nurturing touch while infusing the stone with the warm memories.

6. Sometimes children will ask to pick out a stone for you to keep as well. In this case, the previous steps apply.

7. Write one word on the stone that best represents a characteristic of the child that you want to affirm most. Invite the client to look at their stone whenever they need a reminder of all that they accomplished in therapy.

11.7 CAREGIVER KUDOS

DESCRIPTION:

Caregivers are important partners in the therapeutic growth of their children (Goodyear-Brown, 2021). Caregivers are carving out time in the midst of all the other pulls of life to bring their child to counseling. Caregivers often enter the process feeling like failures, and it is important to celebrate their part in their child's graduation from treatment. This activity should be done at the end of treatment in the client's final session.

TREATMENT GOALS:

- Help the client practice giving appreciation to their caregivers
- Celebrate the caregiver's role in the child's therapeutic growth

MATERIALS NEEDED:

- *Caregiver Kudos* template (or other paper, felt, etc.)
- Scissors
- Coloring utensils
- Other decorations, such as glitter glue or sequins, if desired

DIRECTIONS:

1. Ask the client's caregivers to attend the final session to celebrate their child's graduation from treatment (and to share their letters, if you've also asked them to complete the *Love Letters for Later* activity [11.8]). The caregivers can wait in the lobby while you begin the session with the client separately.

2. Ask the client to reflect on the roles that their caregivers have played in their therapy. In some cases, the caregivers may be thanked simply for bringing the client to treatment. In other cases, clients may thank their caregivers for holding hard stories. For example, children who are coming to treatment after disclosing sexual abuse may thank their caregivers for believing them and "not freaking out."

3. Offer the client the *Caregiver Kudos* template (or they can create their own ribbons). Have them write on each ribbon the name of their caregiver (Mom, Dad, etc.) and one statement that says, "Thank you for..."

4. Invite the client to cut out and color/decorate the ribbons as they desire.

5. Reserve time at the end of the session to bring the caregivers in. The client can present the ribbons at this time (and the caregivers can share their letters, if they've completed the *Love Letters for Later* activity).

CAREGIVER KUDOS TEMPLATE

DEAR _____,

Thank you for...

_____

_____

_____

_____

11.8 LOVE LETTERS FOR LATER

DESCRIPTION:

As part of making a meaningful goodbye in a course of TraumaPlay treatment, caregivers are asked to each write a letter for the client. This letter is read as part of the final session. This often becomes an emotional experience, sometimes surprising the caregiver and usually making for a remarkably connected moment.

TREATMENT GOALS:

- Help the caregivers reflect on the growth of their child in treatment
- Help the caregivers verbally affirm the client
- Provide a moment of meaningful connection between the caregivers and child as they say goodbye to the therapist

MATERIALS NEEDED:

- *Love Letter* template and writing utensils

DIRECTIONS:

1. Introduce the activity to the caregivers at least four weeks before the final session and remind them at each session as treatment counts down. Ensure that the caregivers are able to attend the final session, and ask them to bring their completed letters at that time.

2. Explain that the letter is meant to document the original struggles that brought them to treatment, the growth they have seen in their child, and their hopes for the child's future.

3. Offer the *Love Letter* template as an example. Have each caregiver write on their own paper to personalize the letter, and encourage them to use their own words and speak from their hearts. The template is just a guide in case they get stuck or could benefit from more structure.

4. At the beginning of the final session, check that the caregivers have brought their finished letters along. If they haven't (sometimes caregivers forget or run short on time), you can give them paper and markers and ask them to complete their letters in the lobby while you spend the first part of the session making your meaningful goodbye with the client.

5. Protect time at the end of the session for the caregivers to read their letters out loud (and for the client to give them the *Caregiver Kudos* [11.7], if they've completed that activity as well).

6. Encourage the caregivers to put the letters in a special photo album, scrapbook, box of keepsakes, or similar place so the client can reread them at any time.

LOVE LETTER TEMPLATE

Dear _____,

I remember the day we decided to bring you to _____
_____

Back then it was really hard for you/us to _____
_____

I've watched you grow in _____
_____

I've watched you learn how to _____
_____

I've been amazed as you've risked _____
_____

You are now able to _____
_____

It wasn't always _____
_____

But _____
_____

My hope for you is _____
_____

I'll always be here when _____
_____

Love, _____

References

All templates and handouts are available for
download at www.pesi.com/BBSC

Anda, R. F., Felitti, V. J., Bremner, J. D., Walker, J. D., Whitfield, C. H., Perry, B. D., Dube, S. R., & Giles, W. H. (2006). The enduring effects of abuse and related adverse experiences in childhood: A convergence of evidence from neurobiology and epidemiology. *European Archives of Psychiatry and Clinical Neuroscience, 256*(3), 174–186.

Bailey, R. A. (2004). *Conscious discipline.* Loving Guidance.

Bowlby, J. (1988). *A secure base: Parent-child attachment and healthy human development.* Basic Books.

Baggerly, J. N., Ray, D. C., & Bratton, S. C. (Eds.). (2010). *Child-centered play therapy research: The evidence base for effective practice.* John Wiley & Sons.

Byng-Hall, J. (1995). Creating a secure family base: Some implications of attachment theory for family therapy. *Family Process, 34*(1), 45–58.

Chapman, G. D. (1992). *The five love languages: How to express heartfelt commitment to your mate.* Northfield Publishing.

Freymann, S., & Elffers, J. (2004). *How are you peeling? Foods with moods.* Scholastic Paperbacks.

Goodyear-Brown, P. (2010a). *Play therapy with traumatized children: A prescriptive approach.* John Wiley & Sons.

Goodyear-Brown, P. (2010b). *The worry wars: An anxiety workbook for children and their helpful adults.* Author.

Goodyear-Brown, P. (2019). *Trauma and play therapy: Helping children heal.* Routledge.

Goodyear-Brown, P. (2021). *Parents as partners in child therapy: A clinician's guide.* Guilford Press.

Goodyear-Brown, P., & Hyatt, E. (2020). TraumaPlay and EMDR: Integration and nuance in holding hard stories. In A. Beckley-Forest and A. Monaco (Eds.), *EMDR with children in the play therapy room: An integrated approach* (pp. 33–74). Springer.

Gomez, A. (2007). *Dark, bad day… Go away: A book for children about trauma and EMDR.* Author.

Gruber, T., & Kalish, L. (2005). *Yoga pretzels: 50 fun activities for kids & grownups.* Barefoot Books.

Kenney-Noziska, S. (2012). *Techniques-techniques-techniques: Play-based activities for children, adolescents, and families.* Infinity Publishing. (Original work published 2008)

King, N. (2020, June 1). [Video]. *Self-regulation strategy using dice by Heal with Neal.* YouTube. https://www.youtube.com/watch?v=HGaU3v7dzdI

Landreth, G. L. (2012). *Play therapy: The art of the relationship.* Routledge.

Lowenstein, L. (2008). *Assessment and treatment activities for children, adolescents, and families: Practitioners share their most effective techniques* (UK ed.). Champion Press.

Lowenstein, L. (2016). *Creative CBT interventions for children with anxiety.* Champion Press.

MacLean, P. D. (1990). *The triune brain in evolution: Role in paleocerebral functions.* Springer Science & Business Media.

Perry, B. D. (2009). Examining child maltreatment through a neurodevelopmental lens: Clinical applications of the neurosequential model of therapeutics. *Journal of Loss and Trauma, 14*(4), 240–255.

Porges, S. W. (2011). *The polyvagal theory: Neurophysiological foundations of emotions, attachment, communication, and self-regulation.* W. W. Norton.

Schore, A. N. (2003). *Affect regulation and the repair of the self.* W. W. Norton.

Siegel, D. J. (2010). *Mindsight: The new science of personal transformation.* Bantam.

Siegel, D. J., & Hartzell, M. (2013). *Parenting from the inside out: How a deeper self-understanding can help you raise children who thrive.* Penguin.

Van Hollander, T. (2011, June 28). [Video]. *Red light, green light scribble.* YouTube. https://www.youtube.com/watch?v=2ALNTVMo4LU

Winnicott, D. W. (1971). *Therapeutic consultations in child psychiatry.* Basic Books.

Zouaoui, C. (2018). *Healing with creativity: When talking just isn't enough.* Author.